WRITTEN EXPOSURE THERAPY for PTSD

WRITTEN EXPOSURE THERAPY for PTSD

A Brief Treatment Approach for Mental Health Professionals

DENISE M. SLOAN and BRIAN P. MARX

AMERICAN PSYCHOLOGICAL ASSOCIATION
Washington, DC

Published by
American Psychological Association
750 First Street, NE
Washington, DC 20002
https://www.apa.org

Order Department
https://www.apa.org/pubs/books
order@apa.org

In the U.K., Europe, Africa, and the Middle East, copies may be ordered from Eurospan
https://www.eurospanbookstore.com/apa
info@eurospangroup.com

Typeset in Charter by Circle Graphics, Inc., Reisterstown, MD

Printer: Versa Press, East Peoria, IL
Cover Designer: Nicci Falcone, Gaithersburg, MD

Library of Congress Cataloging-in-Publication Data
Names: Sloan, Denise M., author. | Marx, Brian P., author.
Title: Written exposure therapy for PTSD : a brief treatment approach for
  mental health professionals / by Denise M. Sloan and Brian P. Marx.
Description: Washington, DC : American Psychological Association, 2019. |
  Includes bibliographical references and index.
Identifiers: LCCN 2018051702 (print) | LCCN 2018053102 (ebook) | ISBN
  9781433830136 (eBook) | ISBN 1433830132 (eBook) | ISBN 9781433830129
  (pbk.) | ISBN 1433830124 (pbk.)
Subjects: LCSH: Post-traumatic stress disorder—Treatment. | Brief psychotherapy. |
  Exposure therapy.
Classification: LCC RC552.P67 (ebook) | LCC RC552.P67 S58 2019 (print) |
  DDC 616.89/147—dc23
LC record available at https://lccn.loc.gov/2018051702

http://dx.doi.org/10.1037/0000139-000

Printed in the United States of America

10 9 8 7 6 5 4 3

*For Colin—who teaches us every day about patience,
big dreams, hard questions with even harder answers,
and detours that lead to unexpected discoveries
about ourselves and the world around us.*

Contents

Foreword

The availability of evidence-based treatments for posttraumatic stress disorder (PTSD) has changed dramatically over the past 2 decades, driven in part by large allocations of funding to expand the care for service members and veterans returning from the wars in Iraq and Afghanistan, who now routinely receive services not available to past generations of warriors. Two trauma-focused psychotherapies, prolonged exposure (PE) and cognitive processing therapy (CPT), mandated for uniform dissemination across Veterans Affairs (VA) facilities, have become the dominant treatments in the United States. Funding for research, including randomized clinical trials, has also expanded, and since these wars began, the VA and the Department of Defense (DoD) have produced three revisions of the clinical practice guideline for PTSD (in 2004, 2009, and 2017).

The most striking change in the latest VA/DoD PTSD clinical practice guideline, informative to clinical practice internationally, is that medications (particularly those targeting serotonin reuptake) are no longer considered equivalent to trauma-focused psychotherapy for the primary treatment of PTSD. The evidence review suggested that individual trauma-focused psychotherapy produced higher and longer lasting effect sizes than medications.

This foreword was authored by an employee of the United States government as part of official duty and is considered to be in the public domain. Any views expressed herein do not necessarily represent the views of the United States government, and the author's participation in the work is not meant to serve as an official endorsement.

While the increased availability of trauma-focused treatment is good news for service members, veterans, and civilians suffering from the aftermath of trauma, the reality is that progress overall is not as rosy as we would expect after so many years of effort. The foundation for current clinical treatment with PE, CPT, and most other evidence-based trauma-focused therapies involves the same core components delivered over 12 or more 50- to 90-minute sessions, principally repetitive exposure to the traumatic narrative in some fashion and cognitive restructuring or meaning making. The efficacy of these available therapies has not improved over the years due to a number of factors, not the least of which is low engagement among those most in need of services combined with very high noncompletion rates. Efficacious approaches that can be delivered more efficiently and with greater patient satisfaction have been urgently needed for a very long time.

Enter written exposure therapy (WET), the subject of this book, and arguably one of the most exciting developments in traditional trauma-focused psychotherapy for PTSD. WET is the product of more than 15 years of progressive scientific inquiry that explored such domains as the minimum effective dose of exposure therapy, the optimal delivery methods (with multiple nuances), and mechanisms of efficacy, culminating in an exceptional randomized head-to-head noninferiority trial of WET versus CPT. Like many scientific discoveries, the findings were startling, surprising even the principal investigators themselves (the authors of this book).

Noninferiority is a technical term referring to a clinical trial design in which the study is statistically powered to provide reasonable confidence in the equivalence of two treatments. Research has shown that WET is indeed "noninferior" to CPT in efficacy for PTSD (based on both clinician-administered and self-report measures), as well as depressive symptoms, with results holding for a full year after treatment. However, what is most startling is that the results were achieved with about a tenth of the therapist's time. While CPT required 12 individual, face-to-face, hour-long clinical sessions delivered weekly, WET achieved the same outcomes in only five sessions, each of which involved approximately 20 minutes of face-to-face therapy combined with 30 minutes of writing (alone, while remaining in the clinical setting) during which the patient wrote about their traumatic experience. Also startling was the significantly lower dropout rate from treatment for WET participants compared with the CPT group (6% vs. 40%).

Thus, WET is much more than "noninferior." It is a potential game changer in PTSD treatment offering equivalent efficacy in a fraction of the time and with significantly higher patient satisfaction (lower dropouts) than the most commonly used standard evidence-based trauma-focused therapy. Moreover,

WET is already included under the highest treatment recommendation in the 2017 VA/DoD clinical practice guideline based on clinical trials involving WET and other written narrative exposure therapy approaches (including a dismantling study of CPT). Thus, WET can be considered fully evidence-based, on par with CPT, PE, and other trauma-focused treatments. WET is also a uniquely straightforward "off-the-shelf" treatment that licensed mental health professionals can feel comfortable delivering as soon as they have read and digested this manual.

This manual satisfies an urgent need for an effective, time-efficient trauma-focused treatment that does not induce patients to run for the clinic door. The nonproprietary nature of WET, requiring no further training or certification, lends itself to wide dissemination in mental health clinics and potentially other settings, such as primary care (with appropriate mental health consultation). For all of these reasons, this groundbreaking book will undoubtedly become an essential addition to the libraries of mental health professionals who treat patients with PTSD.

Charles W. Hoge, MD
Walter Reed Army Institute of Research
Silver Spring, Maryland

Acknowledgments

We thank David Becker and other staff in the Books Department at the American Psychological Association for their assistance and helpful insights in writing this book. We also thank Dr. Patricia Resick for her collaboration with us in recent years. We appreciate her crucial contributions to our studies comparing written exposure therapy with cognitive processing therapy and discussions we have had about research design and the interpretation of the findings. We also would like to thank Drs. Terry Keane and Danny Kaloupek for their support and encouragement. Their seminal work on assessing and treating veterans with PTSD has been an inspiration to us and many others in developing evidence-based treatments for PTSD. We thank Dr. James Pennebaker whose work on disclosure of emotions through writing captured our imaginations. We greatly appreciate his time and generosity when we first embarked on this long journey. Finally, we would like to express our deep appreciation to the many trauma survivors whom we have treated throughout the years. We have learned so much from them and they continue to inspire us.

WRITTEN EXPOSURE THERAPY for PTSD

INTRODUCTION

Every year, millions of people are exposed to trauma at home, at work, and in war zones and suffer in its wake. Although treatments for posttraumatic stress disorder (PTSD), including prolonged exposure, cognitive processing therapy, and eye-movement desensitization and reprocessing, are effective, many individuals are not able to access them because they often cannot find providers who offer these treatments, because they do not live near a provider who does, or because they cannot afford to take the time off from work or time away from other obligations or pay for 10 to 15 one-hour therapy sessions. Clinicians also confront barriers that impede their ability to offer these treatments competently to their clients. For instance, substantial training is required to learn how to effectively administer the aforementioned PTSD treatments (e.g., attending workshops over several days, followed by close supervision until the provider displays competency in administering the treatment). Even if they do manage to get the required training and certification, clinicians are often not able to use these treatments because of competing clinical demands and limited staff resources. The barriers for both clients and providers underscore the need to identify alternative PTSD treatments that are brief and do not require extensive provider training. In other words, we

http://dx.doi.org/10.1037/0000139-001
Written Exposure Therapy for PTSD: A Brief Treatment Approach for Mental Health Professionals, by D. M. Sloan and B. P. Marx

need treatments for PTSD that are more widely accessible to both providers and clients.

Written exposure therapy (WET) is a brief five-session treatment we developed to meet this need. It is cost-efficient and requires little clinical training compared with other interventions, and it has proven to be effective at treating different types of trauma. We believe that WET is one of the most promising new treatments for PTSD. In response to the large number of requests we have received from clinicians who wish to use this therapy with their clients, we have written this book as a comprehensive WET treatment manual for mental health practitioners.

OVERVIEW OF WET

The first session of WET requires approximately 1 hour, and the subsequent four sessions require approximately 40 minutes each. The core feature of WET is the written trauma narratives that clients complete during each of the five sessions. The first session of the WET protocol is longer than the other sessions because the clinician spends some time explaining what PTSD is, how it develops, and why repeatedly writing about a traumatic experience in a particular manner is beneficial. During the trauma narrative writing, the client writes about a specific trauma event in great detail, describing the emotions and thoughts that were experienced during the event. The writing instructions are scripted to ensure that clients receive the treatment in a highly consistent manner. The writing instructions evolve over the course of the writing sessions, such that clients begin by writing a detailed account of their trauma experience in the earlier sessions and then progress to describing the impact the event had on their life in the later sessions. Clients write about their trauma experience for 30 minutes each session. Then, the therapist has a 10-minute check-in with the client about his or her experiences in writing about the traumatic event (but not about the traumatic event itself). No between-session assignments are given. The brevity of the treatment, both in terms of number of sessions and duration of sessions, in combination with the lack of between-session assignments results in an efficient treatment that is well tolerated by clients and easy for providers to implement.

As is described in Chapter 2, we have conducted studies with a variety of adult trauma survivors (e.g., sexual assault, physical assault, childhood abuse, combat), and these studies show that WET is an efficacious treatment for PTSD. Even though the treatment focuses on writing about one specific event, individuals who have experienced multiple or chronic traumas (e.g., childhood abuse, military combat) can be successfully treated with WET as well. WET has not been tested with individuals under the age of 18 and so we recommend that it be used only with adults. Based on the evidence demonstrating the efficacy of WET to date, it is now recommended as a first-line treatment by the Department of Veterans Affairs and Department of Defense PTSD Clinical Practice Guidelines (Management of Posttraumatic Stress Disorder Work Group, 2017). In all the clinical trials conducted with WET to date, providers have had either master's- or doctorate-level training in clinical psychology as well as experience with other trauma-focused treatments. Consequently, we believe that this book will be most useful to providers who already have a background using trauma-focused treatments.

HOW TO USE THIS BOOK

We recognize that mental health treatment providers with a variety of education and training backgrounds may use this book. Accordingly, we have included chapters at the beginning of the book that provide an overview of the PTSD diagnosis and a brief guide to assessing PTSD. In Chapter 1, we describe contemporary theories underlying currently available evidence-based PTSD psychotherapies, highlight the common elements of these approaches, and describe how these theories apply to WET. In Chapter 2, we describe the research we conducted to better understand the necessary and sufficient components of PTSD treatment and how this work culminated in the development of the WET protocol. We believe that this background information regarding the development of WET will be helpful for readers to better understand why certain features of the treatment should not be changed. In this chapter, we also describe the results of prior research demonstrating that WET is efficacious in the treatment of PTSD.

Chapter 3 focuses on assessing whether a patient has PTSD and determining whether WET is an appropriate treatment. We provide practical information on ways in which PTSD symptoms can be assessed, as well as consideration of how to assess for other mental health problems. We also discuss using WET when a client has symptoms of PTSD but does not appear to meet full diagnostic criteria for the disorder. We describe how assessment should continue to be conducted during the course of treatment to evaluate whether WET is achieving the desired reductions in PTSD symptoms, as well as using assessment at the end of treatment to determine whether additional treatment (whether with WET or another intervention) is needed.

Chapter 4 provides a comprehensive description of the WET protocol and how it should be delivered. It includes session-by-session instructions that should be read verbatim to the client. These instructions are also presented in an appendix at the end of the book so that clinicians can create copies of the instructions and them hand out to clients during sessions. Throughout Chapter 4, we discuss how clinicians should handle a variety of issues that might arise when using the treatment. In addition, we provide examples of how clinicians should approach the check-in process at the end of the writing sessions. Chapter 5 answers frequently asked questions by clinicians regarding the use and delivery of WET. The last chapter in the book, Chapter 6, presents a variety of case examples that demonstrate various principles and potential outcomes of the WET protocol. These case examples address some of the most frequently asked questions we receive from clinicians regarding how to manage specific client scenarios (e.g., what to do with clients who have experienced multiple traumas, clients who dissociate, and clients who are highly reluctant to confront their trauma memory).

Although the book was written as a guide to WET for mental health treatment providers, it can also be used as a resource for graduate students in psychology and social work who are interested in learning more about treatments for trauma survivors. The book is not intended to be used as a self-help resource for trauma survivors, nor is it intended to be a treatment manual for paraprofessionals, because no studies have examined whether WET can be successfully implemented by non–mental health practitioners (e.g., peer counselors). Consistent with Section 2, Competence, of the *Ethical Principles of Psychologists and Code of Conduct* (American Psychological Association, 2017), only licensed mental health treatment providers with appropriate experience and training should use WET.

We hope that readers find this book and the tools it describes useful in their clinical work with trauma survivors. We also hope this book increases the dissemination of and patient access to an efficient PTSD treatment that will hopefully help many trauma survivors with PTSD who want treatment but may have difficulty obtaining it.

1 OVERVIEW OF PTSD AND TRAUMA-FOCUSED INTERVENTIONS

Although most individuals will experience at least one traumatic event in their lifetimes (Goldstein et al., 2016), only a minority will develop posttraumatic stress disorder (PTSD; Breslau, Davis, Andreski, & Peterson, 1991; Kessler et al., 2005). Some individuals appear to be at heightened risk for developing this disorder. For example, the risk of developing PTSD increases with the repeated exposure to traumatic events (Kessler et al., 2005), and women are more than twice as likely as men to be diagnosed with PTSD in their lifetimes (Seedat et al., 2009). Approximately one quarter of military service members deployed to combat areas develop PTSD (Fulton et al., 2015).

Although a relatively small proportion of individuals develop PTSD, this disorder tends to be chronic and associated with debilitating physical illnesses, such as heart disease, Type II diabetes, and gastrointestinal disorders (Schnurr & Green, 2004). PTSD is also related to accelerated aging and premature death (Wolf & Schnurr, 2016). As a result of these physical problems, those with PTSD have greater medical health care visits (Spottswood, Davydow, & Huang, 2017). Individuals with PTSD are also more likely than members of

http://dx.doi.org/10.1037/0000139-002
Written Exposure Therapy for PTSD: A Brief Treatment Approach for Mental Health Professionals, by D. M. Sloan and B. P. Marx

the general population to be diagnosed with mood, anxiety, and substance use disorders (Goldstein et al., 2016; Pietrzak, Goldstein, Southwick, & Grant, 2011). These disorders frequently develop secondary to PTSD. Personality disorders, such as borderline personality disorder, are also highly comorbid with PTSD (Pagura et al., 2010). Notably, suicidal risk is significantly elevated among those with PTSD (Pietrzak et al., 2011; Wisco et al., 2014), and those with PTSD are 6 times more likely to die by suicide than individuals with other mental disorders (Bachynski et al., 2012).

Given the chronicity and debilitating nature of PTSD, it is not surprising that this disorder significantly impacts social, educational, and occupational functioning. It is not uncommon for people with PTSD to lose their jobs, because reexperiencing symptoms, sleep difficulties, and concentration problems make regular work difficult. The resulting financial problems become an additional stressor and may be a contributory factor leading to extreme hardship, such as homelessness. Social relationships are also negatively affected, potentially leading to social isolation. Problems in the family and the loss of significant relationships are not uncommon.

PTSD DIAGNOSTIC CRITERIA

In the fifth edition of the *Diagnostic and Statistical Manual of Mental Disorders* (*DSM–5*; American Psychiatric Association, 2013), PTSD is now included in its own diagnostic category, Trauma and Stress-Related Disorders. The PTSD diagnostic criteria include several components:

- Criterion A, the stressor criterion in which an individual is exposed directly or indirectly to actual or threatened death, serious injury, or sexual violence;

- Criterion B, characterized by intrusion symptoms, such as recurrent unwanted memories, nightmares, flashbacks, and physiological reactions and psychological distress when confronted with reminders of the trauma;

- Criterion C, characterized by avoidance of stimuli (including people, places, cognitions) that are associated with and remind the individual of the traumatic event;

- Criterion D, characterized by negative alterations in cognitions and mood, such as persistent and exaggerated negative beliefs about oneself, others, or the world; distorted cognitions about the cause or consequences of a traumatic event; a persistent negative emotional state; loss of interest or participation in significant activities; a sense of detachment or estrangement from others; and

- Criterion E, characterized by marked alterations in arousal and reactivity, such as irritable or angry behavior, impaired concentration, difficulty sleeping, an exaggerated startle response, and hypervigilance. (American Psychiatric Association, 2013)

To receive a diagnosis of PTSD, an individual must experience an event that meets the definition of a Criterion A stressor and endorse at least one symptom from Criterion B, at least one symptom from Criterion C, at least two symptoms from Criterion D, and at least two symptoms from Criterion E. Symptoms must be present for 1 month or longer, must result in either clinically significant distress or impairment, and must not be due to medication, substance use, or another medical condition.

Recently, a separate and different set of diagnostic criteria was included in the 11th edition of the *International Classification of Diseases* (ICD–11; World Health Organization, 2018). Like the *DSM–5*, PTSD in the ICD–11 can only be diagnosed in the wake of exposure to an extremely threatening or horrific event or series of events. However, unlike the *DSM–5*, the PTSD criteria in the ICD–11 include only the following criteria:

- reexperiencing symptoms in the form of vivid intrusive memories, flashbacks, or nightmares, which are typically accompanied by strong and overwhelming emotions such as fear or horror and strong physical sensations, or feelings of being overwhelmed or immersed in the same intense emotions that were experienced during the traumatic event;

- avoidance of thoughts and memories of the event or events, or avoidance of activities, situations, or people reminiscent of the event or events; and

- persistent perceptions of heightened current threat, as indicated by hypervigilance or an enhanced startle reaction to stimuli such as unexpected noises.

Like *DSM–5*, symptoms must persist for at least several weeks and cause significant impairment in functioning.

Unlike *DSM–5*, ICD–11 also includes a diagnosis of *Complex PTSD*, a condition that is thought to develop after exposure to an event or series of events of an extremely threatening or horrific nature, most commonly prolonged or repetitive events from which escape is difficult or impossible (e.g., torture, slavery, genocide campaigns, prolonged domestic violence, repeated childhood sexual or physical abuse). The disorder is characterized by the ICD–11 symptoms of PTSD but also includes severe and pervasive problems in affect regulation, related to the traumatic event, and persistent difficulties in sustaining relationships and in feeling close to others. The disturbance causes significant impairment in personal, family, social, educational, occupational, or other important areas of functioning.

Regardless of the diagnostic classification system that is used, PTSD is a prevalent and debilitating illness. Fortunately, we have made tremendous progress in the development of effective psychotherapies for PTSD, with the strongest evidence for cognitive-behavioral, trauma-focused treatments. In the following sections of this chapter, we briefly review these treatments, describe their common features, and discuss how these features are present in written exposure therapy (WET).

EVIDENCE-BASED PSYCHOTHERAPIES FOR PTSD AND CRITICAL TREATMENT COMPONENTS

Two recent clinical practice guidelines for treating patients with PTSD were published. Both guidelines reviewed the most recent empirical studies of PTSD psychotherapies and made recommendations accordingly. The 2017 guidelines published by the American Psychological Association strongly recommend the use of the following psychotherapies for adults diagnosed with PTSD: cognitive behavior therapy (Bryant et al., 2011), cognitive processing therapy (CPT; Resick, Monson, & Chard, 2016), cognitive therapy (Ehlers, Clark, Hackmann, McManus, & Fennell, 2005), and prolonged exposure therapy (Foa, Hembree, & Rothbaum, 2007). Brief eclectic psychotherapy (Gersons, Carlier, Lamberts, & van der Kolk, 2000; Lindauer et al., 2005), eye movement desensitization and reprocessing (EMDR; Shapiro, 1989), and narrative exposure therapy (Ertl, Pfeiffer, Schauer, Elbert, & Neuner, 2011; Stenmark, Catani, Neuner, Elbert, & Holen, 2013) are also recommended, but less strongly.

The recently updated clinical practice guidelines from the Department of Veteran Affairs and Department of Defense (Management of Posttraumatic Stress Disorder Work Group, 2017) recommends individual, manualized trauma-focused psychotherapies that have a primary component of exposure and/or cognitive restructuring to facilitate the processing of traumatic experiences. The recommended trauma-focused approaches include prolonged exposure, CPT, EMDR, specific cognitive behavior therapies for PTSD (Blanchard et al., 2003; Bryant et al., 2008; Ehlers, Mayou, & Bryant, 2003; Ehlers et al., 2014; Kubany et al., 2004; Watson & Marks, 1971), brief eclectic psychotherapy, narrative exposure therapy, and written narrative exposure. Written narrative exposure therapy includes several treatment protocols, including WET.

Although there are some differences between the two guidelines, particularly in the strength in which certain therapies are recommended, there is considerable overlap. Many of these treatments share two critical components that are thought to be responsible for the successful treatment of PTSD symptoms: therapeutic exposure and cognitive processing/cognitive restructuring (e.g., Lee, Taylor, & Drummond, 2006; McLean, Su, & Foa, 2015; Resick et al., 2016; Sloan & Marx, 2017).

Therapeutic Exposure

During therapeutic exposure, clients repeatedly confront internal (e.g., memories, sensations) and/or external (e.g., contextual) trauma reminders until they no longer experience clinically significant distress associated with these reminders. For many years, the prevailing assumption was that such repeated confrontation of trauma reminders both during and between therapy sessions produced extinction of a conditioned fear response associated with these stimuli, as indicated by the reduction in distress when subsequently confronted by these stimuli, which in turn was associated with overall PTSD symptom improvements. It is assumed that clients improve if self-reported distress declines during exposure sessions and if exposure to the same stimuli evoke less distress from one session to the next. However, more recent research has led to changing assumptions about how therapeutic exposure works. It is now believed that therapeutic exposure helps to reduce PTSD symptoms through a process known as *inhibitory learning* (Craske, Treanor, Conway, Zbozinek, & Vervliet, 2014). Instead of habituating to trauma cues, during inhibitory learning an individual learns new responses to trauma cues that compete with and prevent old responses. In the context of therapeutic exposure for those with PTSD, instead of experiencing a reduction in fear, the individual learns that he or she can tolerate being confronted by trauma cues. This learned tolerance competes with and inhibits the old responses to trauma cues (i.e., fear and avoidance) and subsequently inoculates him or her against future relapse (i.e., reemergence of clinically significant PTSD symptoms; Bouton, 2004; Craske et al., 2014).

Imaginal exposure is the core component of WET in which clients are asked to repeatedly confront their traumatic memory by writing about the details of the trauma event, as well as describing the thoughts and feelings they experienced during the event. To make sure that there is repeated confrontation of the trauma memory, clients are instructed to select a single trauma memory as the focus of their writing sessions. In Chapter 4, we describe how to address clients who have multiple trauma events (e.g., childhood abuse, combat trauma). As with other exposure-based treatments, we assume that confrontation of trauma memories through writing fosters the development of fear tolerance behaviors.

Cognitive Therapy/Restructuring

In cognitive therapy for PTSD, cognitions, emotions, and meanings related to a given traumatic event are examined. The client often has developed thoughts, feelings, and meanings that are incongruous with the ways in which the event occurred or with regard to other factual information surrounding the event. For instance, a client might hold the belief that he or she could have prevented the trauma from happening despite clear information about the event that would suggest there was very little, if anything, that the client could have done to prevent the trauma. In cognitive therapy, the therapist challenges these incorrect assertions and brings the client's views back in line with factual information.

Notably, there is evidence that cognitive beliefs that are inconsistent with factual information are corrected through repeatedly recounting the trauma experience without the therapist's use of cognitive therapy (Bryant, Moulds, Guthrie, Dang, & Nixon, 2003; Foa et al., 2005). That is, as clients recount the trauma memory, they begin to remember the specific, factual information of the event, which leads to a correction of their previously held beliefs. For instance, clients might believe that they could have stopped the event or prevented its occurrence, thus holding themselves responsible for the incident. As they recount the trauma they recall specific information regarding who was involved in the event and how it unfolded. This recounting leads to a better understanding of their role within the event. Consequently, the belief that they could have prevented the event and are 100% responsible for the event occurring shifts to a more balanced and accurate perspective.

Cognitive restructuring is presumed to be a key mechanism leading to successful outcome in treatments that are primarily cognitive-focused, such as CPT. However, there is also a growing body of evidence indicating that trauma-related cognitions change as a result of imaginal therapeutic exposure and may be as important as inhibitory learning in producing treatment success (Aderka, Gillihan, McLean, & Foa, 2013; McLean, Su, & Foa, 2015; McLean, Yeh, Rosenfield, & Foa, 2015; Zalta et al., 2014). Similarly, cognitive restructuring is likely a critical mechanism for treatment gains observed in WET. Through the repeated recounting of the trauma memory, clients begin to correct their trauma-related cognitions (e.g., "It's my fault that the event happened" restructured to "I did everything I could to prevent the event from happening. Other people were responsible for the event"). The writing sessions for WET begin with instructing clients to write about the details of the traumatic event, but later sessions instruct clients to examine how the traumatic event has affected their lives and the meaning of it. In doing so, clients' beliefs shift such that they become more factual and less distorted.

HOW WET CAN ADDRESS COMMON BARRIERS TO PTSD TREATMENT

Although several PTSD treatments are recommended by the clinical practice guidelines, these treatments are not effective for everyone who receives them. Typically, one third still meet criteria for PTSD following treatment (Bradley, Greene, Russ, Dutra, & Westen, 2005) and approximately a third drop out of these treatments prematurely (Imel, Laska, Jakupcak, & Simpson, 2013). Factors related to the client, the therapist, and the contexts in which treatment is conducted can reduce the effectiveness of these treatments or prevent them from working altogether. However, WET can address many of these barriers.

Client Factors

Avoidance of traumatic reminders is a cardinal symptom of PTSD, and, as such, the nature of the disorder makes it particularly difficult for those with the condition to engage in many of the best treatments. Avoidance can take several forms (substance use, other addictive behaviors, distraction, social isolation), with each presenting its own unique challenges in therapy. Regardless of form, efforts to avoid trauma reminders can result in dropping out prematurely from PTSD treatment. Studies find dropout rates between 18% and 65% for CPT and prolonged exposure, depending on treatment setting (randomized controlled trial vs. treatment in a clinic; Garcia, Kelley, Rentz, & Lee, 2011; Hembree et al., 2003; Imel et al., 2013; Kehle-Forbes, Meis, Spoont, & Polusny, 2016).

It is generally thought that clients do not show for their therapy appointments and drop out of treatment altogether because exposure to trauma-related material brings about unwanted feelings and thoughts related to the trauma. This conjecture is supported by research findings indicating that attrition typically occurs early in the course of treatment (Gutner, Gallagher, Baker, Sloan, & Resick, 2016; Kehle-Forbes et al., 2016), when clients are preparing to begin or have just begun therapeutic exposure exercises.

As in these other trauma-focused treatments, clients who receive WET are exposed to reminders of their traumas. Yet, low dropout rates are observed for WET (i.e., less than 10%; Sloan, Marx, Lee, & Resick, 2018). What accounts for this striking difference between WET and other trauma-focused treatments in treatment dropout? As readers will soon see when we review the WET protocol in Chapter 4, there may be several reasons for the low attrition. First, unlike other trauma-focused treatments, the therapeutic exposures occur in writing and do not include a recounting of the traumatic experience to the therapist. This arrangement may allow clients to feel more comfortable and better tolerate the exposures. Second, unlike in other trauma-focused treatments where the exposures do not begin for several sessions until after initial preparatory work has been completed, WET starts exposure in the first session. Clients in other therapies may become fearful about how difficult the exposure might be, and this fear may lead them to drop out prior to starting the exposure sessions. In contrast, by conducting the exposure in the first session the client learns that the imaginal exposure is not as aversive as what they might have feared and that they are able to tolerate the exposure. Indeed, the therapist ends the first session with the observation that the most difficult session has just ended. Third, in contrast to other trauma-focused treatments, there are no between-session assignments. Other trauma-focused treatments include between-session assignments such as writing about the traumatic experience in the absence of a therapist, listening to a session recording in which the client recounted the traumatic experience out loud to the therapist, or confronting previously avoided and feared situations related to the trauma. Compliance with these between-session assignments is highly variable, and clients report difficulty in completing or attempting to complete these assignments. Accordingly, clients can develop feelings of shame or guilt related to uncompleted assignments. Uncompleted assignments may be an indicator of avoidance of trauma cues. The shame or guilt associated with uncompleted assignments may further promote avoidance of trauma reminders and lead to missed sessions or even treatment dropout. The pattern of not completing homework followed by treatment session no-shows or cancellations disrupts treatment progress and ultimately is related to poorer treatment outcome (Gutner, Suvak, Sloan, & Resick, 2016). Because there are no between-session assignments in WET, there are no opportunities for clients to experience shame or guilt associated with these assignments. Thus, these conditions further promote consistent treatment attendance and subsequent completion of the treatment in 5 weeks (Sloan, Marx, & Lee, 2018).

Therapist Factors

Therapist factors also play a significant role in the effectiveness of a given treatment. One important factor is the extent to which therapists are trained to use these treatments. Opportunities to learn evidence-based treatments may be limited. For example, the American Psychological Association's Division of Clinical Psychology (Division 12) lists only four training sites for learning prolonged exposure and only two for learning CPT. Of note, many of these are training sites where early career clinicians may choose to train. Although options for training exist for professionals (e.g., workshops followed by consultation), clinicians must often seek them on their own and bear the financial costs associated with receiving training in these protocols. The financial costs may be considerable, because training workshops are typically two to three full days followed by approximately 20 consultation meetings during which consultation is provided for two cases. Beyond these barriers, therapists may be reluctant to learn evidence-based treatments, particularly exposure-based treatments, or to use them in their practices, for a variety of reasons. These include fear of worsening symptoms, fear that the client may dissociate during the session, and concerns about treatment dropout (Becker, Zayfert, & Anderson, 2004).

To be clear, not unlike any other psychosocial treatment, training is needed to successfully deliver WET. However, the time and cost of the training are substantially less than that needed for other trauma-focused treatments. Specifically, WET workshops typically require 6 hours and can be conducted via video teleconferencing rather than in person. Follow-up consultation is needed to successfully deliver WET, but because of the short duration of the treatment, fewer consultation calls are needed (generally no more than 10 consultation meetings).

Contextual Factors

Broader, systems-level issues also arise, particularly with respect to costs. First, properly training clinicians in evidence-based treatments can be costly (Herschell, Kolko, Baumann, & Davis, 2010). It may also be challenging to assure that clinicians are adhering to treatment protocols or that they continue to use these treatments, particularly after a given training period has ended (Becker et al., 2004; Herschell et al., 2010). WET may be a particularly appealing treatment option for health care systems given the decreased time needed to train providers. The cost associated with training is also less. Moreover, health care systems would likely find the reduced number of treatment sessions of WET appealing because a greater number of clients can be treated in a shorter amount of time. Treatment adherence to WET is generally high given that the majority of the treatment sessions are scripted.

Implementation Barriers

Recognizing the increased need for PTSD treatment services resulting from post-9/11 conflicts, the Department of Veteran Affairs and the Department of Defense devoted considerable resources to disseminate CPT and prolonged exposure to mental health providers in their respective settings (Eftekhari et al., 2013). This widescale dissemination effort was a major undertaking spanning many years. Providers who were interested in being trained in these treatments were required to attend intensive workshops (e.g., 2 days) followed by supervision for at least two cases (treated to completion) using the specific manualized protocol within one year of attending the workshop. However, because treatment dropout can be high among clients receiving prolonged exposure and CPT, the supervision period often lasts many months (Kehle-Forbes et al., 2016). Once these criteria were met, providers received certification. Many providers received certification in both treatments, whereas some providers received certification in just one treatment.

Following several years of disseminating these treatments, a number of studies have examined the implementation of these treatments in Veterans Affairs and Department of Defense health care settings. Findings from these studies revealed that providers believe that prolonged exposure and CPT are effective treatments but that they use supportive counseling models more frequently than prolonged exposure or CPT (Finley et al., 2015; Watts et al., 2014). Moreover, providers report using some but not all of the treatment components for both approaches (Borah et al., 2013; Watts et al., 2014), which is problematic because it is unknown if these treatments are effective when they are changed unsystematically. Providers reported that although they believe that prolonged exposure and CPT are effective, they either alter these treatments or use supportive care instead because of clinical care demands and limited staff resources (Borah et al., 2013; Finley et al., 2015).

Because WET is a brief treatment, it is less affected by these implementation barriers, and more clients can be treated with limited staff resources. In addition, because the WET protocol is highly structured and scripted, there is less chance that providers will deviate from the protocol, thereby potentially increasing treatment outcome success among those clients receiving the treatment.

Taken together, a number of PTSD treatment options have overlapping features. The efficiency and structure of WET addresses many of the challenges that have been raised with other evidence-based PTSD treatment approaches. In Chapter 2 we describe how WET was developed and present research findings to support its use to treat PTSD.

2 DEVELOPMENT AND EFFICACY FINDINGS OF WRITTEN EXPOSURE THERAPY

Our work that ultimately resulted in the written exposure therapy (WET) protocol began out of curiosity about the wide-ranging benefits associated with an expressive writing procedure studied by Pennebaker and Beall (1986). This procedure involves writing about stressful or traumatic experiences for 20 minutes a day on three consecutive days. To our surprise, and despite the procedure's brevity, numerous published studies have demonstrated its robust physical and psychological health benefits (for a review, see Frattaroli, 2006). As we read the results of these studies, we were struck by their consistency as well as by the apparent similarities between Pennebaker and Beall's protocol and exposure-based therapies for posttraumatic stress disorder (PTSD). However, we assumed that the expressive writing procedure would not be beneficial for individuals who had experienced an event that qualified as a bona fide traumatic stressor (Criterion A traumatic event; American Psychiatric Association, 1994, 2013) and PTSD symptoms of at least moderate severity, because it did not include as many sessions as exposure-based treatments typically do (i.e., three writing sessions vs. 12 therapy sessions).

We tested this hypothesis in our first study by randomly assigning individuals who reported exposure to a PTSD Criterion A traumatic stressor and

http://dx.doi.org/10.1037/0000139-003
Written Exposure Therapy for PTSD: A Brief Treatment Approach for Mental Health Professionals, by D. M. Sloan and B. P. Marx

PTSD symptoms of at least moderate severity to either an expressive writing condition or a control writing condition in which individuals wrote about how they spent their time each day with no emotions or opinions (Sloan & Marx, 2004). To ensure that we replicated the expressive writing procedure, we obtained the protocol directly from Pennebaker and consulted with him over the course of this study as well as subsequent studies testing the extent to which the expressive writing protocol would be helpful to those with trauma histories and accompanying PTSD symptoms. To test the assumed mechanism of action of therapeutic exposure (i.e., fear extinction), we collected saliva samples from participants before and after each writing session to examine salivary cortisol reactivity as well as self-report ratings of emotional reactivity. The inhibitory learning model was not yet widely adopted. We expected to find no between-group differences in PTSD symptom change because we assumed that the expressive writing protocol did not include enough writing sessions (i.e., exposures) to result in the extinction of the pathological fear response.

In contrast to our expectations, we found that participants assigned to the expressive writing condition reported a significant reduction in PTSD symptom severity at both immediate posttreatment and later follow-up, relative to those assigned to the control condition. Moreover, consistent with the extinction model, salivary cortisol and self-reported ratings of emotional reactivity indicated initial activation of the fear response during the first expressive writing session following by extinction of fear responding by the third session (Sloan & Marx, 2004).

These findings surprised us because we assumed that individuals would require more writing sessions (i.e., a larger treatment dose) for extinction of pathological fear responding. Subsequently, we examined the empirical literature in an attempt to uncover studies that had demonstrated the necessary and sufficient therapy dose for successful PTSD treatment. Incredibly, in doing this literature review, we found that no prior studies had examined the association between therapy dose and treatment outcome for PTSD.[1] This discovery, in combination with the findings from our first study, led us to conduct a series of subsequent studies to better understand the critical components for successful PTSD treatment.

In our next study, we examined whether it was necessary to write about the same traumatic experience during each writing session for successful

---

[1] We examined the literature in 2002 and at that time there were no published studies investigating the dose needed for successful PTSD outcome. However, there are now several publications addressing this issue (e.g., Galovski, Blain, Mott, Elwood, & Houle, 2012; Nacasch et al., 2015; van Minnen & Foa, 2006).

outcome (Sloan, Marx, & Epstein, 2005). Pennebaker and Beall's (1986) original expressive writing protocol permits switching between different stressful or traumatic events, and, consequently, some individuals do change topics between the writing sessions. Such an allowance is inconsistent with what is typically done in PTSD exposure-based therapy protocols, which generally require that a client be repeatedly exposed to reminders of the same trauma so that extinction can occur. That being said, there has been some controversy regarding the specificity of the exposure stimuli, with some researchers (e.g., Watson & Marks, 1971) suggesting that any stimulus can be used during exposure sessions, as long as those stimuli elicit intense negative affect from the individual. If this is the case, then expressive writing should produce positive results regardless of whether the individual changes topics as long as whatever the individual writes about elicits sufficiently strong negative affect. To determine whether this was indeed the case, we recruited participants who had a history of multiple traumatic stressor exposures and reported at least moderately severe PTSD symptoms.

We randomly assigned participants to write about the same traumatic event during each session, write about different traumatic events during each session, or write about their day without any emotions or opinions (the control writing condition). All other expressive writing procedures were followed. We also collected salivary cortisol reactivity data during each session and self-reported emotion ratings to test the extinction of fear responding hypothesis. Findings indicated that only those who wrote about the same traumatic event during each session reported significant reductions in PTSD symptom severity at posttreatment and follow-up assessments. Individuals assigned to write about different traumatic events during each session and the control condition reported no significant reduction in PTSD symptom severity. An important observation was that participants in both trauma writing conditions displayed elevated fear responding during the first writing session, but only those who wrote about the same trauma displayed a significant extinction of fear responding by the third writing session. In fact, individuals who wrote about different traumas during each session displayed significantly greater fear response during the third session, relative to participants assigned to the same trauma writing condition and the control writing condition (Sloan et al., 2005). These findings underscore the importance of writing about the same trauma during each session and the importance of the specificity of exposure stimuli (i.e., trauma event) when conducting imaginal exposure.

We then conducted several additional studies to investigate possible moderators of expressive writing outcomes, as well as to continue to examine critical components of expressive writing, such as writing instructions that emphasize the expression of emotion versus emphasizing the thoughts experienced during the trauma event (Sloan, Marx, Epstein, & Lexington, 2007). For instance, we found that men and women obtained equal benefits from expressive writing (Epstein, Sloan, & Marx, 2005), individuals with brooding rumination style reaped greater beneficial outcome associated with expressive writing than those not prone to a brooding ruminative style (Sloan, Marx, Epstein, & Dobbs, 2008), and individuals with better emotion regulation ability (as indexed by respiratory sinus arrhythmia) achieved better outcomes associated with expressive writing than individual with poorer emotion regulation ability (Sloan & Epstein, 2005). We also found that emphasizing emotion expression in the instructional set for expressive writing led to greater benefits relative to instructions emphasizing cognitive restructuring (Sloan et al., 2007). The findings of these studies led us to better understand for whom expressive writing may be beneficial and under what conditions it might be most beneficial.

After spending approximately eight years examining the critical components of the expressive writing protocol, we next investigated whether it would be beneficial for individuals with a diagnosis of PTSD (Sloan, Marx, & Greenberg, 2011). In our prior studies, we had asked participants to provide self-report ratings of PTSD symptoms instead of conducting a diagnostic interview. Given the range of self-reported PTSD symptoms across the studies, we certainly had included some individuals who would have met the diagnostic criteria for PTSD as well as individuals who did not have PTSD. Thus, it was unclear whether expressive writing would promote clinically significant symptom reductions among individuals with greater PTSD severity.

To address this question, we conducted a study in which we assessed for PTSD using a clinician-administered interview. Participants with a confirmed PTSD diagnosis were randomly assigned to either an expressive writing condition or a control writing condition. Based on our earlier findings (Sloan et al., 2005), we altered the expressive writing protocol to instruct individuals to write about the same traumatic experience during each session. We continued to test the underlying mechanism of exposure (i.e., extinction) by examining heart rate reactivity and self-reported emotion ratings during each session. Findings indicated that expressive writing was not associated with a significant reduction in PTSD symptoms, and the two conditions did not significantly differ in PTSD symptom severity at posttreatment and follow-up assessments. Heart rate and self-report emotion reactivity data indicated initial activation of fear responding for participants assigned to the expressive writing condition, but no subsequent reduction in this response was observed following the first session (Sloan et al., 2011).

These findings among those diagnosed with PTSD were what we had expected to observe in our very first study. However, we were glad that we did not conduct this study first because we would not have learned as much about what does and does not work when using narrative writing to treat posttraumatic stress symptoms. Our systematic research provided data to support the notion that therapeutic imaginal exposure through written narratives could be an efficacious treatment, but we needed to make modifications for it to be beneficial for individuals with more severe PTSD. We made several modifications that were informed by data from our prior studies, our pilot work that we conducted to further determine the sufficient narrative writing dose, and other relevant empirical data.

First, we changed the number and duration of writing sessions included in the protocol based upon some pilot work we conducted to investigate the optimal narrative writing dose necessary and sufficient for successful treatment outcome. This pilot work indicated that five sessions, each of which includes 30 minutes of writing, was a sufficient dose for successful outcome with individuals diagnosed with PTSD.

Next, we altered the instructions for writing based on our cumulative empirical work (e.g., Sloan et al., 2007) and on the empirical literature. For example, the protocol instructs the client to write about his or her traumatic experience using a distanced perspective ("as you look back upon it now") rather than an immersed perspective ("write about it in the present tense, as if it were happening right now"). This decision was informed by a rich body of research indicating that people are better able to accurately recount and "work through" highly negative life events when using a distanced versus immersed perspective (for a review, see Kross & Ayduk, 2011, 2017).

As a final modification, we added a psychoeducation component, something that all evidence-based treatments for PTSD include (e.g., Hamblen, Schnurr, Rosenberg, & Eftekhari, 2009), and we included a treatment rationale to the first treatment session. It is important to inform clients about the core symptoms of PTSD as well as how PTSD develops and is maintained. This information provides an appropriate context for describing the treatment rationale (i.e., why writing about one's traumatic experiences will reduce PTSD). There are clear data showing that treatment buy-in accounts for substantial variance in treatment outcome (e.g., Addis & Carpenter, 2000). It is also important to explain to clients why you are asking them to do the very thing they have made great efforts not to do in order for them to be willing to write about their traumatic experiences.

For each of the treatment sessions, we scripted the protocol to enable easy dissemination across providers and to ensure that the treatment was the same regardless of the therapist implementing the treatment. Thus, we intend for the therapist to read (verbatim) the treatment information to the client. We have not scripted the sections of the treatment that are individualized for a specific client, such as providing feedback regarding how well clients followed writing instructions and checking in with clients about how the writing session went for them. These individualized portions of the protocol are described in detail in Chapter 4.

Following these changes, we named the new protocol *written exposure therapy*. Since developing the protocol, we have conducted several studies investigating its efficacy.

INITIAL EFFICACY STUDY

Although we believed that WET would be beneficial in treating PTSD, it was important to test this speculation. As an initial test of the efficacy of the treatment, we compared WET with a waiting-list comparison condition with funding we received from the National Institute of Mental Health. At the request of the funding agency, we also included a telehealth comparison condition in which individuals would receive WET at home. This was a reasonable suggestion given WET's format. That is, WET would seem to be an ideal treatment to conduct outside of a clinic, making the treatment that much more accessible to those in need of treatment.

We tested WET with a sample of adults who had PTSD resulting from a motor vehicle accident. We selected this sample for several reasons. First, motor vehicle accidents are the most common type of traumatic stressor that results in PTSD (Blanchard & Hickling, 2004). Second, we believed it would be best to conduct the initial efficacy test of WET with a sample of individuals who had PTSD resulting from a singular, discrete traumatic event rather from a recurring traumatic event, such as childhood abuse or combat exposure.

Before we conducted the randomized controlled trial, we had to first conduct pilot work to develop a protocol for the telehealth version of WET. In an effort to make sure that we could engage participants in WET outside of the clinic, we structured the sessions such that we scheduled specific days and times that each session would be conducted. A therapist would then call the individual at the specified time for each session and provide the instructions for writing during that session. The participant would be reminded that the session had to be completed in 30 minutes, at which time the therapist would call back to check in regarding how the writing session went. Sadly, we encountered two major problems with the telehealth pilot. First, a substantial percentage (i.e., at least 50%) of the participants who initially agreed to receive telehealth WET dropped out prior to the first treatment session.

This high percentage of dropouts was strikingly different from what we typically had observed in any of our previous expressive writing studies. The second problem we encountered was that most of the people who received at least one telehealth WET session reported engaging in other activities during the writing session, such as taking phone calls or checking e-mail. A substantial number of individuals who engaged in at least one telehealth session of WET also dropped out. This observation was consistent with the high number of treatment dropouts among those receiving telehealth writing interventions in other studies (e.g., Lange et al., 2003). We understood this unwillingness of participants to comply with the writing protocol as avoidance of trauma reminders and associated distress. Certainly, avoidance is a central feature of PTSD (American Psychiatric Association, 2013; World Health Organization, 2018), and avoidance has deterred individuals with PTSD from engaging in other trauma-focused treatments, such as prolonged exposure (PE) and cognitive processing therapy (CPT; Hoge & Chard, 2018). Individuals with PTSD are seemingly much more willing to comply with the WET protocol when they are in the clinic than outside the clinic. In addition, participants have told us that they would be reluctant to receive WET at home for fear that they may not be able to manage the negative affect that would be elicited by the writing sessions. They report feeling that they have a "safety net" within the clinic. Because of the difficulty we experienced with piloting the telehealth version of the WET protocol, we ultimately dropped telehealth WET from the randomized controlled trial.

We then proceeded with the first efficacy study of WET using a randomized controlled trial design in which 46 participants with a diagnosis of motor vehicle accident-related PTSD were randomly assigned either to WET or a waiting-list control condition (Sloan, Marx, Bovin, Feinstein, & Gallagher, 2012). In keeping with our goal to determine the mechanism through which WET reduced PTSD symptoms, we collected self-report emotion ratings and recorded heart rate during each writing session. Our findings indicated that, compared with participants assigned to the control condition, those assigned to WET reported a significant reduction in PTSD symptom severity at posttreatment, and symptom reduction was maintained 3 and 6 months later. Moreover, only one of 23 WET participants (5%) continued to meet diagnostic criteria for PTSD at the 3-month follow-up relative to 15 of 23 waiting-list participants (75%). The treatment was well tolerated, with only two individuals (7%) dropping out of treatment prematurely. In addition, as a group, WET participants reported that they were highly satisfied with the treatment ($M = 28.20$, $SD = 3.3$, out of a maximum possible total score of 32).

We found support for the assumption that fear habituated during the WET procedure. Specifically, we observed a significant reduction in self-reported emotion ratings for participants assigned to WET between the treatment sessions (Sloan et al., 2012), and treatment gains were significantly associated with initial physiological activation and between-session extinction as indexed by self-reported arousal ratings (Wisco, Baker, & Sloan, 2016).

Study participants completed the Driving and Riding Avoidance Questionnaire (Clapp et al., 2011) during the study, and we used those data to examine whether changes occurred in driving and riding avoidance behaviors, the most common type of avoidance behavior among individuals with motor vehicle accident-related PTSD (Blanchard & Hickling, 2004). Although we did not assign or discuss in vivo exposure sessions with participants, we did observe significant reductions in driving and riding avoidance-related behaviors from baseline, as well as a significant reduction relative to participants assigned to the waiting-list condition (Baker, Litwack, Clapp, Beck, & Sloan, 2014). The finding of confronting other PTSD-related avoidance behaviors may be the result of the information regarding importance of avoidance in maintaining PTSD introduced in the first treatment session and/or the positive experience participants had with the imaginal exposure sessions. For example, when asked why they would have spontaneously started driving on highways again after avoiding these behaviors since their accident, participants would remark that since they were able to confront the trauma memory they felt that they could also confront other things that they had been avoiding related to their trauma experience. Importantly, we noted that the between-treatment condition effect that we obtained is similar to that reported for CPT and PE therapy when using a no treatment comparison condition (Cahill, Rothbaum, Resick, & Follette, 2009; Cusack et al., 2016).

EFFICACY STUDY COMPARING WET WITH CPT

Although the study outcomes were encouraging, we had compared WET with only a waiting-list comparison condition. Additional work with more rigorous study designs were needed to ascertain whether WET produces clinically significant, sustainable reductions in PTSD symptoms that are comparable with the reductions in PTSD symptoms produced by other evidence-based treatments, such as PE and CPT. Thus, we believed the next best step in investigating the efficacy of WET would be to directly compare WET with one of the first-line treatments for PTSD using a noninferiority randomized controlled trial (for details regarding the study design, see Sloan, Marx, & Resick, 2016).

We decided to compare WET with CPT for two reasons.[2] First, CPT includes written trauma accounts, to be written between sessions and then brought into the session to be read aloud to the therapist. We believed that the inclusion of written trauma accounts using a different format would allow for an interesting comparison. The second and more compelling rationale to include CPT was that Dr. Patricia Resick worked at our institution when we started the study, and she agreed to be responsible for training and supervising the CPT therapists. Having Dr. Resick overseeing the CPT therapists would ensure that participants assigned to this condition would receive the treatment from highly competent, well-trained therapists. Our primary hypotheses were that WET would be noninferior to CPT, despite the substantial differences in treatment dose (five sessions vs. 12 sessions), and that there would be a significantly greater treatment dropout in CPT relative to WET based on dropout data previously reported for the two treatments (e.g., Resick, Nishith, Weaver, Astin, & Feuer, 2002; Resick et al., 2008; Sloan et al., 2012).

Participants in the study were 126 men and women diagnosed with PTSD (Sloan, Marx, Lee, & Resick, 2018). We included PTSD resulting from any traumatic event in order to increase generalizability of the findings. Our hypothesis that WET would be noninferior to CPT was confirmed. Specifically, we found that the mean difference in Clinician-Administered PTSD Scale–5 (CAPS-5; Weathers et al., 2013a) scores between participants who received WET and participants who received CPT was no greater than 4.3 points at all posttreatment and follow-up assessments. This difference was far less than the previously established noninferiority margin of 10 points for the CAPS. We also found that a significantly greater number of individuals dropped out prematurely from CPT (39%) relative to WET (6%). Dropout differences were not likely attributable to the longer treatment duration for CPT because the majority (76%) of individuals who dropped out of CPT did so within the first five sessions. Additionally, we collected information regarding reasons for treatment dropout; it is possible that some individuals may have dropped out of CPT prematurely because they believed they achieved treatment gains and did not perceive the need for additional treatment sessions. Only one person who dropped out of CPT prematurely did so for this reason. Of note, the noninferiority findings were also observed when examining the treatment completer sample (Sloan, Marx, & Lee, 2018).

---

[2] It should be noted that we use the term *cognitive processing therapy* to refer to the full protocol that includes both written accounts and cognitive restructuring, as has been the practice until recently. Resick and colleagues (2016) now refer to a protocol that includes only cognitive restructuring as CPT, and the term CPT+A is used to refer to the protocol that includes written accounts.

Treatment process measures were also examined, including treatment expectancy, treatment satisfaction, and therapeutic bond. No significant treatment differences were observed in terms of satisfaction with the treatment or treatment expectancy (Sloan, Marx, Lee, & Resick, 2018). Using the short form of the Working Alliance Inventory (Hatcher & Gillaspy, 2006), we investigated whether there was greater therapeutic bond for CPT, which is what we assumed given the greater amount of time that the therapist spends with the participant. Contrary to our expectations, there were no significant differences in the reporting of the therapeutic bond by therapists and participants in both conditions. Thus, although therapists spend considerably less interaction time with clients in WET than in more traditional individual psychotherapies, the therapeutic bond does not appear to suffer.

In a follow-up paper, we reported that the treatment gains observed for both WET and CPT were maintained at a long-term (i.e., 60 weeks) follow-up assessment (Thompson-Hollands, Marx, Lee, Resick, & Sloan, 2018). We also found a significant reduction in depression symptoms occurred for both treatments, with no significant between-group difference observed (Thompson-Hollands et al., 2018).

Does WET Work Better for Some People Than Others?

A secondary, exploratory goal of this study was to investigate moderators of treatment outcomes for both treatment conditions. Given the dose difference between the two treatments, one might assume that WET would not work as well with clients who are experiencing more severe symptoms (e.g., greater PTSD symptom severity, greater number of psychiatric comorbid diagnoses, longer duration of time since trauma event) or who have multiple traumatic experiences. In addition, because of the focus on writing in the treatment, clinicians frequently ask whether clients' education levels influence WET treatment outcomes. Although we understand why clinicians ask this question, it is important to recognize that the quality of the writing (e.g., spelling, sentence structure, grammar) does not matter. Rather, writing is used as a means of confronting one's traumatic memory. Grammar, sentence structure, and overall quality of writing do not matter because they should not impede one's ability to write about the details of his or her traumatic event. Nonetheless, because clinicians frequently asked whether educational background and verbal ability influences treatment outcomes, we also included a measure of estimated IQ as a potential moderator of treatment outcomes in this study.

We examined a number of other potential moderator variables, including demographic characteristics (sex, age, racial background, educational level;

Marx, Sloan, Lee, & Resick, 2017). To our surprise, we did not find that baseline PTSD severity, number of comorbid diagnosis, depression severity, or time since trauma event moderated PTSD treatment outcome for either CPT or WET. We also did not find that any demographic variable moderated treatment outcome. The only variable that did moderate treatment outcome was estimated IQ, with higher baseline estimated IQ scores being associated with better treatment outcomes for CPT. Notably, individuals with lower estimated IQ scores who received CPT also showed significant improvements in PTSD symptoms, but those with higher estimated IQ scores showed even larger symptom improvements. Estimated IQ scores at baseline were not associated with PTSD symptom changes among participants who received WET. Thus, the efficacy of WET is not affected by diagnostic severity or number of past traumatic events. WET outcome is also not affected by intelligence or educational level.

Efficacy Studies With Military Veterans and Active Duty Service Members

The previously described findings come from studies of predominantly civilian samples; we thought it would be important to also investigate trauma-focused treatments with military veterans and active duty service members. Indeed, although PE and CPT have the strongest empirical support for PTSD treatments (Management of Posttraumatic Stress Disorder Work Group, 2017), much of the efficacy and effectiveness data for PE and CPT has been obtained with civilian samples. The recent conflicts in Iraq and Afghanistan have resulted in a substantial increase in veterans and service members presenting for PTSD services (Tanielian & Jaycox, 2008). This increased demand for care has also resulted in recognition of the need to conduct studies investigating the efficacy of first-line treatments with veterans and service members. As summarized by Steenkamp, Litz, Hoge, and Marmar (2015), the available evidence indicates that PE and CPT do not work as well with military veterans and service members as they do with nonveteran civilians. Specifically, Steenkamp et al. reported that studies examining the efficacy of PE or CPT with service members or veterans found that 49% to 70% of study participants achieved clinically meaningful symptom reductions and that 60% to 72% of participants retained their PTSD diagnosis following either PE or CPT. This is in contrast with approximately 80% of nonveteran civilian participants achieving clinically meaningful reductions and only approximately one third of participants retaining their PTSD diagnosis following treatment with PE or CPT (Steenkamp et al., 2015).

In addition to the concerns regarding the effectiveness of CPT and PE with veterans and service members, as previously described in Chapter 1, there is emerging evidence suggesting that Veterans Affairs and Department of Defense providers are infrequently using first-line PTSD treatments even after receiving training in PE and CPT (Borah et al., 2013; Finley et al., 2015; Watts et al., 2014). Taken together, these findings suggest the need for additional treatment options with better treatment retention and greater efficiency.

To examine the feasibility, acceptability, and initial efficacy of WET with veterans, we first conducted an open pilot with a small sample ($N = 7$; Sloan, Lee, Litwack, Sawyer, & Marx, 2013). The findings from this small study were promising. Specifically, only one of the seven veterans dropped out of treatment prematurely; this is a relatively low treatment dropout rate for veterans seeking trauma-focused treatment (Kehle-Forbes, Meis, Spoont, & Polusny, 2016). Moreover, five of the seven veterans reported clinically significant reductions in PTSD symptoms at their follow-up assessments to assessors who used a structured clinical interview. Notably, veterans reported good to excellent treatment satisfaction ratings (Sloan et al., 2013).

We also examined veterans in the recently published clinical trial in which WET was directly compared with CPT (Sloan, Marx, Lee, & Resick, 2018). We have not published the findings for the subset of veterans because it is a small group and, as such, not appropriately powered to examine between-treatment condition differences. Nevertheless, we provide descriptive results of the veteran subsample here to shed additional light on treatment engagement and treatment outcomes for WET with military veterans. A total of 33 veterans were enrolled in the study and were randomly assigned to CPT ($n = 16$) or WET ($n = 17$). Of the veterans assigned to both treatments, only one (6%) dropped out of WET whereas eight (50%) dropped out of CPT. The most commonly reported reason veterans dropped out of CPT was that the treatment was too difficult (e.g., homework assignments too time-consuming and complicated; sessions were causing an increase in trauma-related thoughts, which were causing distress).

Veterans assigned to both CPT and WET showed substantial reductions in PTSD symptom severity, with a mean treatment outcome CAPS-5 score of 22.25 ($SD = 6.5$) and 21.82 ($SD = 7.2$) for CPT and WET, respectively. Completer data are of particular importance given that 50% of the veterans randomized to CPT dropped out prematurely. Notably, among the veterans who completed treatment, the between-group difference in mean CAPS-5 change was the same, with the largest between-group difference at any assessment interval being just 1.12 points. These findings suggest that even though WET may include substantially fewer treatment sessions than CPT, it may result in greater treatment retention and similar treatment outcomes among veterans with PTSD. Although promising, caution should be taken when interpreting these findings because of the small number of veterans included in the study.

Taken together, the findings from these two studies suggest that WET is well tolerated by military veterans, and our efficacy findings are promising. We currently have a grant application under review to conduct an efficacy study of WET with a large sample of veterans seeking treatment in the Veterans Affairs health care system. Conducting such a study is important to establish that WET is efficacious in the treatment of veterans diagnosed with PTSD.

In terms of studying the efficacy of WET with military service members, with funding from the Department of Defense, we are currently investigating whether WET is noninferior to CPT, cognitive only protocol (CPT-C; Resick et al., 2016) in a sample of active duty service men and women diagnosed with PTSD.[3] We are using a cognitive only protocol of CPT because this treatment protocol removes the trauma narrative account component of CPT, and there is some evidence that this protocol results in faster treatment gains relative to the original CPT protocol (Resick et al., 2008). Once again, we expect that WET will be noninferior to CPT-C despite the difference in treatment dose. We are also expecting to find a significant difference in treatment dropout with fewer dropouts in WET. The recruitment phase for this study is in progress; as a result, we are unable to provide information on treatment outcome or dropout at this time.

Summary of Efficacy Findings

The efficacy findings obtained to date suggest that WET is an efficacious and well-tolerated efficient treatment for individuals diagnosed with PTSD. Treatment dropouts have been consistently low, which is notable given that treatment dropout for trauma-focused treatments tend to be relatively high (i.e., 36%; Imel et al., 2013). It is unlikely that the brief nature of the treatment explains the low dropout rate, given that most individuals drop out of other trauma-focused treatments early in the course of treatment (e.g., Gutner, Gallagher, Baker, Sloan, & Resick, 2016; Kehle-Forbes et al., 2016), and this was the pattern of dropout that we observed in our noninferiority study (Sloan, Marx, Lee, & Resick, 2018). Participants also report high levels of satisfaction with the treatment.

---

[3] Cognitive processing therapy, cognitive only used to be referred to as CPT-C (Resick, Monson, & Chard, 2014). However, Resick and colleagues (2016) now refer to CPT-C as CPT. In this chapter we use the term CPT-C to refer to CPT, cognitive only.

The outcome findings reported by Sloan et al. (2012) suggested that symptom reductions may be similar to those observed with first-line PTSD treatments, and findings from our recently completed noninferiority study further indicate that this is the case. The results of the noninferiority study are notable given the substantially larger treatment dose in CPT. Moreover, treatment gains for WET are maintained at long-term follow-up (Thompson-Hollands et al., 2018). As with our earlier work, these findings underscore the importance of examining the necessary and sufficient elements of treatment to maximize outcomes while simultaneously making treatments efficient for both clients and providers.

Although we have found WET to be noninferior to CPT in one study, additional investigation is needed. Nonetheless, even if WET is observed to be inferior to CPT or other first line PTSD treatments, there may still be merit in using WET because of low treatment dropout and cost-effectiveness considerations. For instance, if substantially fewer clients drop out of WET relative to other trauma-focused treatments, it may be preferable to use WET to ensure high treatment retention and delivery of adequate treatment dose. In terms of cost-effectiveness, WET is a cost-effective treatment option for clients given the total number of sessions in combination with the lack of between-session assignments. Cost-effectiveness is also important from the clinician perspective. For the mental health provider, first-line PTSD treatments can be time-consuming when considering the amount of training and supervision needed to become certified in these treatments (e.g., Karlin et al., 2010). In addition, clinicians require some preparation time before each session when delivering PE and CPT. This can include making copies from the manual needed for the upcoming session and reviewing prior session content. In terms of preparation for WET treatment sessions, the clinician must read the trauma narrative completed in the last session so that he or she can provide feedback for the upcoming session; this preparation typically requires approximately 5 minutes. Moreover, initial training and subsequent supervision for WET is minimal (Sloan et al., 2016); in contrast, initial training and follow-up consultation for PE and CPT are extensive (Karlin et al., 2010).

FUTURE DIRECTIONS

Given that WET is scripted and there is less therapist–client interaction than in PE, CPT, and other trauma-focused treatments, one might assume that nonclinicians or paraprofessionals could deliver the intervention. This is an important question to address because each of the studies conducted to date used therapists who have at least a master's-level degree in psychology but more often have a doctoral degree in clinical psychology. In addition, the therapists have experience with trauma-focused treatments more generally. Given the large number of individuals in need of treatment services, many of whom do not present to mental health clinics for treatment (Kazdin, 2017), it is essential to identify treatments that can be readily disseminated and implemented by a wide variety of professionals. At present, we have no information about the level of training and experience needed to successfully implement WET, but this is an important question to examine.

Another important direction for future investigations is gaining information on the implementation of WET. It would be valuable to know when and why clinicians in various settings elect to use WET. Also, knowing how and why clinicians might modify the intervention would provide valuable information in terms of understanding how the treatment might be used in routine care clinics and the manner in which alterations to the protocol are deemed necessary. Such alterations in routine care settings may lead to greater efficacy findings for the treatment.

One might assume that WET could be used as a telehealth treatment. However, as we already described, our experience with a telehealth version of the WET protocol indicates that WET might not work well outside of the clinic. Nevertheless, additional work should be devoted to investigating WET as a telehealth treatment given the critical need to reach a greater number of individuals in need of trauma treatment. One way in which WET may be successfully delivered remotely is with the use of video teleconferencing. If a clinician was able to remain in contact with the client via video teleconference while he or she completed his or her narrative writing, then there may be better treatment compliance than what we previously observed when using telephone calls to monitor participant adherence.

The use of an efficient and easily implemented PTSD treatment also has appeal for primary care clinics. The percentage of PTSD among clients presenting for primary care services is higher than the rate in the general population (Spottswood, Davydow, & Huang, 2017). Notably, individuals with PTSD are more likely to present to primary care for services than to mental health care clinics (Kazdin, 2017). Thus, it is important to treat these clients for PTSD within the primary care setting. In that setting, it is not possible to provide time-intensive PTSD treatments. However, given its brevity, WET may be an ideal treatment to be used within the primary care environment.

In recognition of the need to increase the reach of mental health treatments, we have been collaborating with Dr. Trey Andrews III at the University of Nebraska, who has created a Spanish-translated version of the WET protocol. Dr. Andrews is currently testing the efficacy of the Spanish-translated version of WET with a sample of Spanish-speaking women who are survivors of domestic violence and, so far, the results look promising. We eagerly await the final results when the study is completed.

3

ASSESSING PTSD BEFORE BEGINNING WRITTEN EXPOSURE THERAPY

Before delivering written exposure therapy (WET), clinicians should first determine whether a client has posttraumatic stress disorder (PTSD), whether other psychiatric conditions may be present, and whether WET is an appropriate treatment. In this chapter, we describe how to construct an appropriate PTSD assessment battery, describe many important considerations that may influence the decision to use WET, and discuss the importance of monitoring client progress over the entire course of WET. Our discussion in this chapter of assessment within the context of the WET protocol is not intended to be comprehensive in its evaluation of all instruments available for the assessment of PTSD. Rather, the intent is to provide a heuristic structure that clinicians might find helpful to use when selecting an instrument or set of instruments for clinical purposes.

http://dx.doi.org/10.1037/0000139-004
Written Exposure Therapy for PTSD: A Brief Treatment Approach for Mental Health Professionals, by D. M. Sloan and B. P. Marx

ASSESSMENT BEFORE BEGINNING TREATMENT

Assessment of PTSD

Although considerable attention has been given to identifying treatments for PTSD, much less attention has been given to the role of assessment in the successful treatment of PTSD. Careful assessment is crucial to identifying an appropriate treatment (e.g., treatment for PTSD vs. depression), monitoring treatment progress, and determining whether additional treatment is needed. Several well-designed and psychometrically sound self-report scales and interviews are available for assessing the presence and severity of PTSD. That being said, it is critical to remember that all measures have inherent limitations. In making choices about which measures to use, it is necessary to consider the strengths and limitations of an available measure, the extent to which measures have demonstrated clinical utility (e.g., time, cost-effectiveness), and psychometric properties (i.e., reliability, validity, types of samples on which measures have been normed, cut scores).

Because the diagnosis of PTSD requires exposure to a traumatic event, exposure to such events should first be evaluated. Similarly, as WET requires the client to write about an extremely upsetting, traumatic experience that is directly related to his or her presenting symptoms, a history of exposure to at least one such event is necessary. Numerous self-report instruments are available to assess exposure to various potentially traumatic events. A good example of such a measure is the Life Events Checklist (LEC-5; Weathers et al., 2013b) for the *Diagnostic and Statistical Manual for Mental Disorders, Fifth Edition* (*DSM–5*; American Psychiatric Association, 2013), which gathers information on exposure to 16 events known to potentially result in PTSD and includes one additional item assessing any other extraordinarily stressful event not captured in the first 16 items. Respondents indicate varying levels of exposure to each type of potentially traumatic event on a 6-point nominal scale, and they may endorse different types of exposure (e.g., directly experienced, witnessed) to the same trauma type. The LEC-5 does not yield a total score or composite score and is often used in combination with other measures (i.e., the Clinician-Administered PTSD Scale–5; Weathers et al., 2013a) to determine whether the respondent meets the PTSD Criterion A (stressor criterion).

Once exposure to a potentially traumatic event is established, the presence and severity of symptoms resulting from the traumatic event should be assessed. Structured diagnostic interviews by a well-trained clinician are widely considered to be the gold standard for PTSD diagnostic status and symptom severity. Developed by the National Center for PTSD (Blake et al., 1990; Weathers et al., 2013a), the Clinician-Administered PTSD Scale (CAPS) is one of the most widely used structured interviews for diagnosing and measuring the severity of PTSD (Weathers, Keane, & Davidson, 2001). This measure also has strong psychometric properties (Weathers et al., 2018). The CAPS was initially developed for the fourth edition of the *Diagnostic and Statistical Manual of Mental Disorders* (*DSM–IV*; American Psychiatric Association, 1994), and an updated version has been developed for the fifth edition (*DSM–5*; American Psychiatric Association, 2013; CAPS-5). On the CAPS-5, frequency and intensity are assessed and then combined for one overall severity score for each item. The CAPS-5 promotes uniform administration and scoring through carefully phrased prompt questions and explicit rating scale anchors with clear behavioral referents. The CAPS-5 has past week, past month, and worst month (i.e., lifetime) versions. Administration time is approximately 30 to 60 minutes, depending on the extent to which symptoms are reported by the respondent.

We recognize that treatment providers may not always have the time or training needed to administer the CAPS-5 when determining the presence and severity of PTSD. In such cases, clinicians should be thoughtful about how to best proceed, because a good, thorough assessment of PTSD symptoms prior to treatment initiation is typically necessary to determine whether treatment is indicated. In addition, the assessment is imperative to know what traumatic event to focus on during treatment and whether the client received any benefits after treatment is provided.

In cases in which it is not possible or practical to administer a CAPS-5, clinicians should first consider using other, less time-intensive interview measures, such as the PTSD module from the Structured Clinical Interview for *DSM–5* (First, Williams, Karg, & Spitzer, 2016) to ensure that all diagnostic criteria are queried appropriately. In certain other instances, it is possible to use self-report measures that are administered with the instruction to anchor all symptoms to a particular traumatic stressor. After the client has completed the self-report instrument, the clinician should take some time to review the client's responses with him or her and query for clarification wherever necessary. Even still with this more thorough approach, self-report instruments are able to provide only a provisional PTSD diagnosis that should be confirmed, whenever possible, with a more rigorous assessment method. Many if not all PTSD self-report measures ask questions in a similar fashion, use similar rating scales, and have sound psychometric properties. Still, we recommend that clinicians consider the available psychometric data for the population on which it is to be used. In doing this, clinicians are maximizing the accuracy and efficiency of the selected measure. Although self-report measures can be used to gauge PTSD symptom severity and provide a provisional PTSD diagnosis when time and resources are scarce, they may be more vulnerable than diagnostic interviews to response bias.

A review of all available PTSD self-report measures is beyond the scope of this chapter. However, we describe one psychometrically sound and widely used self-report PTSD measure. Developed by researchers at the National Center for PTSD (Weathers, Litz, Herman, Huska, & Keane, 1993), the PTSD Checklist (PCL) is a self-report measure of PTSD symptoms that is most frequently used in the trauma field. The scale has been recently revised to reflect the diagnostic symptoms outline in the *DSM–5* (PCL–5; Weathers, Litz, et al., 2013). Different scoring procedures may be used to yield either a continuous measure of symptom severity or a dichotomous indicator of diagnostic status. Dichotomous scoring methods include an overall cutoff score, a symptom cluster scoring approach, or a combination of the two. Respondents are asked to rate, on a Likert scale, "how much each problem has bothered them" during the past month. The time frame can be adjusted as needed to suit the goals of the assessment. The measure requires approximately 5 to 10 minutes to complete and has strong psychometric properties (e.g., Bovin et al., 2016).

As of this writing, we are not aware of any well-validated diagnostic or self-report instruments that correspond exclusively to the *International Classification of Diseases, 11th revision* (ICD–11) diagnostic criteria for PTSD and Complex PTSD (World Health Organization, 2018). This presents a challenge for clinicians using the ICD–11 diagnostic criteria. Until such measures are developed and validated, we recommend using the *DSM–5* corresponding instruments as their developers prescribed and then use the acquired information accordingly.

Assessment of Psychiatric Comorbidity

The presence of one or more comorbid conditions with PTSD can complicate treatment planning. The overlap among symptoms of PTSD with conditions such as depression, substance use disorders, postconcussive syndrome, and anxiety disorders requires thorough assessment to accurately attribute an individual's symptoms to a specific disorder and to determine the best course of treatment. Comprehensive diagnostic procedures that rely upon structured or semistructured diagnostic interviews facilitate identification and diagnosis of comorbid conditions that can be incorporated into treatment planning.

Without appropriate additional assessment for other co-occurring disorders, the presence of certain hallmark PTSD symptoms, such as nightmares, dissociative flashbacks, exaggerated startle, or hypervigilance, may lead clinicians to overlook the possibility that the presence of additional disorders may be important for determining the best course of treatment. Inadequate assessment of comorbidities may also lead to misspecification of treatment targets. Though current clinical practice guidelines generally recommend treating PTSD and psychiatric comorbidities concurrently, treatment of PTSD may need to be delayed, or referral to specialty care may be necessary for individuals with high levels of suicidality or severe co-occurring disorders (e.g., severe substance use disorders, active psychotic disorders; Management of Posttraumatic Stress Disorder Work Group, 2017). Thus, a sound understanding of these co-occurring psychiatric conditions and their manifestation in the presence of PTSD is essential.

Numerous diagnostic interviews and self-report instruments can be used to assess psychiatric comorbidity, and it is beyond the scope of this book to review them. However, some commonly used instruments are the Structured Clinical Interview for *DSM–5* (First et al., 2016), the Patient Health Questionnaire (Kroenke & Spitzer, 2002), the Beck Depression Inventory–II (Beck, Steer, & Brown, 1996), and Minnesota Multiphasic Personality Inventory—2—Restructured Form (Ben-Porath & Tellegen, 2011). Clinicians should always choose additional measures appropriately and according to the manner in which they were intended to be used.

During the course of conducting assessment, a number of presenting features should also be assessed that will help to determine the best course of treatment and potential issues that may arise when delivering WET.

Factors That May Influence Case Conceptualization and Treatment Planning

Trauma Type

People can experience a wide range of potentially traumatic events. For example, involvement in combat, a sexual assault, or a motor vehicle accident all qualify as potential Criterion A events, given the exposure to actual or threatened death, serious injury, or sexual violation. However, the degree to which certain PTSD symptoms may be prominent among survivors of these different experiences may have important implications for case conceptualization and treatment planning. For example, survivors' guilt may be prominent for a combat veteran, dissociative symptoms might be more likely for a sexual assault victim, and conditioned fear of driving might be a serious problem for a motor vehicle accident survivor. These differential aspects of individual cases with PTSD can be particularly valuable in case conceptualization and understanding how a client might respond to the writing sessions in the WET protocol or the particular aspects of the trauma on which the client should focus during the writing. To date, there is no evidence that WET works better for any specific type of trauma survivor than others (Marx, Sloan, Lee, & Resick, 2017). Over the course of our work with WET, we have observed that WET works equally well for individuals with a variety of trauma exposures, including those whose trauma involves multiple exposures (e.g., child-hood sexual abuse, military combat). As we describe in a case study in Chapter 6, WET has been successfully delivered with clients who present with dissociative symptoms and when guilt is a prominent feature of a client's presentation.

Developmental Factors

Despite the absence of evidence for treatment effects specific to age (e.g., Foa, Keane, Friedman, & Cohen, 2008), age variables are important for case conceptualization and treatment planning. A 30-year-old adult seeking treatment for PTSD secondary to childhood sexual abuse that occurred at age 10 is likely to present very differently from a 40-year-old seeking treatment for a sexual assault that occurred at age 20. In both cases, 20 years have passed since the trauma; however, the individual who was victimized at age 10 presumably coped using strategies that were developmentally appropriate for a child (at least initially), whereas the individual victimized at age 20 presumably coped using strategies that were developmentally appropriate for a young adult. Such developmental factors may have a significant impact on the way each individual initially processed the trauma, how he or she continues to experience it (e.g., specific dissociative symptoms), and how he or she may write about it during the writing sessions.

The length of time since trauma exposure may also be relevant from the standpoint of remembering some of the details of what happened. Although memories for the central aspects of traumatic experiences typically remain intact and trauma memories tend to be stronger than memories of more every-day experiences, it is quite common for trauma survivors to forget peripheral, often inessential details of the experience. Poor memory for these less important details should not be confused with avoidance of trauma reminders, and the clinician should work with the client to determine which details are most relevant and should therefore be the focus of the writing sessions and which details are less critical to the writing process. The WET protocol requires that the individual remembers these essential details of the event and can provide these details to the therapist in writing. It is fine if the client does not remember some of the less essential details, such as the exact date and time the event occurred, names of others who were present, or what happened in the immediate aftermath of the experience. Sometimes, forgetting details can indeed indicate active attempts on the part of the client to avoid trauma reminders. In these cases, a careful, thorough assessment can help clients recall important aspects of the trauma. In instances where the client continues to have memory gaps even after a careful assessment, we have observed that these gaps often get filled as the client writes about the experience. The extent to which the previously unrecalled details that get filled in during the writing are accurate can be unclear to both the clinician and the client. However, clinicians should not be overly concerned about this. We have observed that these clients usually are more bothered by their inability to recall these details than by concerns about the accuracy of the details they subsequently provide, and they experience some relief from simply being able to close a memory gap. Clinicians should weigh the benefit of the relief provided by closing this memory gap against the accuracy of these newly recalled details.

Cultural Considerations

The generalizability of methods used to assess PTSD is a function of several features of the assessment setting and client characteristics. Culture, language, race, age, and gender are factors that might influence the use and the interpretation of results from both structured diagnostic interviews and self-report measures. Attention to these variables is essential to discerning the presence or absence of PTSD.

We recommend that clinicians consider the samples on which an assessment instrument for PTSD was validated when selecting a measure. The need to develop instruments that are culturally sensitive has been of great interest for many years because of documentation of ethnocultural-specific responses to traumatic events. For example, researchers have provided evidence of differences in the reported risk for and severity of PTSD symptoms in Caucasians and ethnic minorities following a traumatic event (Alcántara, Casement, & Lewis-Fernández, 2013; Roberts, Gilman, Breslau, Breslau, & Koenen, 2011). Furthermore, there is substantial variation in the prevalence of PTSD across the world. Even across similarly low-income and developing nations recovering from conflict (which have high rates of trauma exposure and vulnerability factors), rates of PTSD vary widely (de Jong et al., 2001), suggesting the importance of considering unique contextual factors in the development and use of PTSD assessment instruments.

To date, evidence-based psychological assessment of PTSD has evolved primarily within the context of Western, developed, and industrialized countries. Thus, PTSD assessment may be limited by a lack of culturally sensitive measures and by the tremendous diversity among cultural groups of interest (Marques, Robinaugh, LeBlanc, & Hinton, 2011). However, there has been progress in developing culturally sensitive measures. For example, the CAPS has been studied among culturally different groups with excellent success (e.g., Charney & Keane, 2007).

USING ASSESSMENT DATA TO DETERMINE WHETHER WET IS RIGHT FOR YOUR CLIENT

After determining that the client's PTSD symptoms should be the focus of treatment, clinicians should carefully examine the additional data acquired during the assessment to determine whether WET is an appropriate course for treatment. As previously mentioned, we do not recommend using WET with clients who experienced a trauma for which they have no memory or some scarce details of the event (e.g., trauma in early childhood that they have no memory of and are only aware of the trauma occurring due to the reports of others). For those clients who are unconscious for part of the entire trauma (e.g., lost consciousness as a result of a head injury, blacked out from substances), clinicians can use WET to focus on the parts of the event that they do recall. As previously mentioned, in these cases it is not unusual for these clients to fill in memory gaps as they recount the memory in writing, especially if these gaps were created by chronic avoidance of the trauma memory.

Consistent with the guidelines for other trauma-focused treatments, we would not recommend using WET if there is risk of ongoing trauma, such as domestic violence. In such situations it is more important to ensure client safety first. Once the client is out of harm's way, then he or she can begin treatment.

We would also be cautious about using WET with clients who have expressed strong reservations about confronting their trauma memories. In such cases, the clinician should empathize with the client, demonstrate that he or she understands the reluctance, and explain why continuing to avoid the memory will only perpetuate the client's suffering and how confronting the memory in the manner described by the WET protocol ultimately will be helpful. If the client continues to be resistant or reluctantly agrees but then displays avoidance during the first few treatment sessions by not following the writing instructions (noncompliance) or by not attending therapy sessions, then the clinician and client should discuss if it would be in the best interest to change course and try a non–trauma-focused treatment, such as present-centered therapy.

We do not recommend using WET if the client is unable to write in the primary language of the clinician. The clinician must be able to comprehend the trauma narrative to make sure the instructions are being followed. In addition, the client must be able to understand the treatment rationale and instructions for writing in order for the treatment to be beneficial.

If PTSD is not the primary problem or diagnosis causing impairment, then a treatment that targets the primary problem area should be considered. Once the primary problem has been addressed, WET can be reconsidered if the client continues to report that PTSD symptoms are causing impairment even after the primary issue has been resolved. By the same token, WET can be helpful in cases in which the client has some, but not all, of the requisite *DSM–5* or ICD diagnostic criteria to warrant a PTSD diagnosis. Indeed, individuals with partial (or sub) PTSD experience significant distress and dysfunction that can benefit from intervention. WET may be the ideal treatment for such individuals because of its brevity.

There is no evidence to indicate that other trauma-focused treatments should not be provided to clients with concurrent suicidal ideation, substance use, depression, Axis II disorders, or complex PTSD presentations (De Jongh et al., 2016; Gradus, Suvak, Wisco, Marx, & Resick, 2013; van Minnen, Harned, Zoellner, & Mills, 2012), and this is the case for WET as well. These commonly occurring comorbid conditions may be driven by the presence of PTSD. Thus, treating PTSD may also treat these comorbid conditions (van Minnen, Zoellner, Harned, & Mills, 2015). However, as previously stated, if a client has a severe substance use disorder or is actively psychotic, these issues should be addressed first before starting WET. Once the client's condition has been stabilized, WET can be implemented. Similarly, if a client is determined to be a high suicide risk or an imminent danger to others, then these issues should be addressed first through either hospitalization or development of a proper risk management plan (Bryan et al., 2018).

The presence of dissociative symptoms should not automatically deter a clinician from using WET. However, if the dissociative symptoms are more severe than the PTSD symptoms and cause more interference, then the treatment of dissociative symptoms or disorders should take precedence over the treatment of PTSD.

Assessment During WET

Once a clinician has determined that a client has PTSD and decides to use WET to treat that disorder, continued monitoring of symptoms throughout the course of treatment is important. By assessing PTSD symptoms during treatment, the clinician can determine whether the treatment is working. Assessing PTSD symptoms on a weekly basis is ideal because the clinician can monitor symptom changes (increases or decreases) and use the information to provide the client with additional feedback about treatment progress. Brief self-report measures that do not overburden the client, such as the PCL-5, are ideal for monitoring treatment progress from week to week.

Assessment during treatment can also help the clinician gauge clients' level of engagement. Clients receiving WET often report mild symptom exacerbation after their first writing session, and we typically view this mild exacerbation as evidence of engagement in the treatment. There may be several explanations for why a client may not show any symptom increase during the first sessions of WET. One possible explanation may be that the client is not fully engaged or participating in the treatment, either because it is too painful (e.g., effortful avoidance) or because he or she is unable to engage because of dissociative or other inhibiting processes. If the client is, in fact, not engaging, this is important information for the clinician. This information can only be gleaned by assessment that takes place during treatment.

In addition to the assessment of PTSD during treatment, the assessment of distress during the treatment session can also provide important information. For instance, we typically use the Subjective Units of Distress Scale (SUDS; Wolpe, 1958) to assess client engagement and/or distress before and after the narrative writing portion of the WET session. Most often, the SUDS is a scale from 0 to 100 for measuring the subjective intensity of disturbance or distress currently experienced by an individual. Used within the WET protocol, the client is prompted by the clinician to provide a SUDS rating at the beginning and end of each writing session. As described in the next chapter, a significant reduction in SUDS ratings from the first to the last WET session is significantly related to successful PTSD treatment outcome (i.e., significant reduction in PTSD symptoms).

Assessment at the End of Treatment

Assessment of outcomes at the end of treatment should bring the clinician and the client full circle, by again assessing diagnostic change from pretreatment to posttreatment and identifying remaining problem areas. Ideally, the clinician and the client should repeat the initial diagnostic measure that was administered before treatment started, to determine the extent of change in symptom frequency and severity. Posttreatment assessments can also provide information about symptoms or conditions, such as depression, that may require additional intervention. It is not uncommon for depression symptoms to significantly decrease during WET (Thompson-Hollands et al., 2018), and anxiety and substance use also typically decreases with treatment of PTSD. However, if substantial comorbid symptoms persist despite treatment gains in PTSD, the clinician should consider targeting this area(s) next.

SUMMARY

We have discussed the assessment of PTSD for the purposes of determining the presence and severity of PTSD and whether WET is an appropriate treatment option and incorporating best practices in PTSD assessment. We also placed emphasis on clinical feasibility in the use of these measures.

With respect to assessment for diagnosis, we emphasize the importance of the clear identification of a Criterion A event, to which subsequent symptom endorsements are linked. We also recommend structured or semistructured diagnostic interviews when possible, in particular those that assess frequency and intensity of symptoms, such as the CAPS-5. For the purposes of case conceptualization and treatment planning, a broader assessment of contextual factors, including psychiatric comorbidity and exposure to other potentially traumatic events, provides valuable adjunct information. We further recommend regular brief assessments of symptoms for the purposes of treatment monitoring and a repeated diagnostic assessment at the end of WET to determine whether treatment was beneficial and whether additional symptom areas should be targeted.

4 DELIVERY OF WRITTEN EXPOSURE THERAPY AND SPECIAL CONSIDERATIONS

As described previously, written exposure therapy (WET) is a five-session treatment; the first session requires approximately 60 minutes to complete, and the remaining four sessions require approximately 40 minutes each. The treatment protocol is included in the appendix to this book. The material in the appendix is given to clients when delivering WET. This material includes information that is read to clients in each session. We provide the writing instructions to clients so they can refer to them in each session as they complete the writing, and all of the session materials are available to clients after leaving treatment. In this way, the treatment can become a coping tool that clients can use in the future should the need arise. In this chapter, we repeat the script of each session so that the structure and content of each session is clear, as well as instructions for what to do before and after the script is read to the client. The chapter also provides guidance for how to present the treatment and how to manage potential problems that may arise when implementing the treatment.

http://dx.doi.org/10.1037/0000139-005
Written Exposure Therapy for PTSD: A Brief Treatment Approach for Mental Health Professionals, by D. M. Sloan and B. P. Marx

STRUCTURE OF TREATMENT

Before describing the specifics of conducting each session, it is important to provide some general information about the structure of the treatment.

Reading the Instructions to Clients Verbatim From the Script

As described in Chapter 2, WET is the product of years of rigorous research and development. This line of work has led to a very precise and optimized method for delivering the treatment protocol. As such, it is critical that the directions for each writing session be read verbatim to the client. The instructions should not be changed or rephrased. In addition to ensuring that WET is delivered in the manner in which it is intended, reading the instructions verbatim ensures that every person receives the treatment in the same standardized manner. Following the procedures increases the likelihood of success. However, the wording can be modified slightly to make it more specific to the client. For instance, instead of stating "the trauma event," the clinician should state the specific event that the client has identified as the focus of the treatment (e.g., the sexual assault, the car accident). Similarly, when describing sights and sounds related to the event, the clinician should use examples that the client has described in relation to their trauma experience rather than the generic examples in the script.

Importance of Writing for the Full 30 Minutes During Each Session

The clinician should emphasize that the writing works best when the person follows the instructions, fully engages in the writing, and writes for the full 30 minutes that he or she is allotted. In the unlikely event that the client completes the writing assignment before the writing time ends, he or she should be reminded to begin writing the narrative all over again, starting at the beginning. Often, people will recall more details of the trauma as they continue to write, and clients frequently comment that the 30 minutes went by faster than they expected. Nonetheless, there is no reason for the person to stop writing before the allotted 30 minutes. Also, no breaks during the writing are permitted, and the client should be instructed to turn off all personal electronics (e.g., cell phones, Apple watches, tablets, laptops) and eliminate all distractions (e.g., no listening to music while writing). The goal is to be fully focused on the writing for the entire 30 minutes devoted to the trauma narrative.

Context of the Narrative Writing

In our efficacy studies of WET, we have left clients alone while they write. However, this is often not possible, or even permitted, in some clinical settings. In such instances, it is perfectly acceptable for the therapist to remain in the room with the client during the writing. It may even be beneficial to ensure that the client is fully focused on the writing instead of checking a cell phone, putting on headphones to listen to music during writing, or simply stopping the writing before the allotted 30 minutes. However, if the clinician remains in the room, the client should be instructed not to stop writing to talk with the clinician. Providers can let the client know that they will be busy with paperwork or other activities while the client is writing and they will also be turning their backs to the client to quietly work. The clinician should be careful not to make too much noise (e.g., by using a computer keyboard), which would distract the client. The main point is to emphasize that the client should be fully focused on the writing, even if the clinician remains in the room.

Ideally, the client will have a desk or table on which to write; a clipboard would also suffice. The client should also be provided with several sheets of lined paper and a pen. The clinician should keep track of time and inform the client that he or she will be doing that so that the client is not keeping track of the time while writing.

Interval Between Sessions

In our early work on expressive writing, we followed Pennebaker and Beall's (1986) protocol, which calls for participants to write on several consecutive days. Although this schedule worked well with our study participants, this approach varies from typical clinical practice in which clients meet with their therapists once a week for 50 minutes. Accordingly, we have conducted all of our WET efficacy studies using weekly sessions. Based on our work to date, we recommend that therapists who use WET do so in the context of weekly or even more frequent sessions (e.g., twice per week) with their clients. Less frequent WET sessions may not provide optimal conditions for symptom change to occur. Clinicians should also emphasize the importance of regular session attendance with their clients. Cancellations and no-shows will extend the length of the treatment as well as prevent inhibitory learning. Clients who need to reschedule a session should try to do so as soon as possible (even within the same week) to remain on track to complete WET in 5 weeks. In general, posttraumatic stress disorder (PTSD) trauma-focused treatment works best when clients regularly attend their treatment sessions (Gutner, Suvak, Sloan, & Resick, 2016).

Selection of the Trauma Event

As described in Chapter 3, the source of the PTSD symptoms (i.e., index event) will have been established along with the severity of PTSD symptoms as part of the assessment protocol. In instances in which the client has a clear, discrete event that is connected to symptoms, he or she should be directed to write about that specific experience during all writing sessions. It is common for trauma survivors to have been exposed to more than one trauma and some traumas, such as childhood sexual abuse or combat, occur over an extended period of time during which several discrete experiences may be especially upsetting. In such cases, PTSD symptoms may be related to different events, and it may be challenging for clients to choose a particular event on which to focus during the writing because they cannot decide which experience is the most upsetting one (e.g., "they're all bad"). In such cases, the clinician should work closely and diligently with the client to choose a specific experience on which to focus during the writing. This is because our prior work shows that WET works best when the individual writes about the same discrete experience during each writing session.

To select the specific event, clients should think about the experience that causes them the most distress or is tied most closely to their avoidance symptoms (i.e., the event they try to avoid reminders of the most often or the one that is the most difficult to avoid reminders of, despite attempts to do so). If clients report that no one single event stands out for them, but instead a handful of events are prominent, then the clinician should inquire whether the memory for one of these events is particularly clear; this is the event that should be selected. If several events are equally vivid, then any one of these events can be selected. Clients should also be reassured that they will have the opportunity to write about the series of events more broadly in later writing sessions.

Indexing Distress Levels

As described in Chapter 3, we assess client discomfort using the Subjective Units of Distress Scale (SUDS; Wolpe, 1958) just before he or she starts writing and again immediately when writing ends. Indexing client distress level is helpful in measuring how anxious clients are before each writing session, how engaged they are during the writing session, and whether or not their distress level drops across the course of the WET sessions. Client distress is rated on a scale from 0 to 100, with 0 representing no distress at all (so relaxed one could fall asleep) and 100 representing the most distressed one has ever felt in his or her lifetime. It is important for the clinician to explain the SUDS rating and how to gauge ratings in the first session so that the client is providing the best possible estimate of his or her distress. It is not unusual for high SUDS ratings to be given before and after the first writing session, and high SUDS ratings may continue to be reported after completing the second and possibly even the third sessions.

Do not be concerned about high SUDS ratings just before the start of the first writing session. Such high levels typically reflect anticipatory anxiety in advance of confronting the trauma memory for the first time. SUDS ratings at the start of the writing may remain high at the start of the second session, but a gradual decrease should be observed across the five sessions. We discuss how best to use the SUDS ratings when we describe the check-in process following the narrative writing.

CONDUCTING SESSION 1

It is helpful for the clinician to let the client know in advance that the instructions will be read by the clinician verbatim to ensure that the client is receiving the treatment as it was intended. The client should be told that the clinician will first be providing some general information about symptoms of PTSD, how PTSD symptoms are maintained, and why writing about their traumatic experience will be beneficial in treating PTSD. The following text should be read aloud to the client.

> Survivors of traumatic experiences often go through changes in their physical reactions, emotions, thoughts, and behaviors in the wake of such experiences.
>
> Examples of changes in physical reactions may include increased fatigue, nausea (feeling sick to your stomach), sweating or chills, shock, dizziness, chest pains, trouble breathing, and numbness.
>
> Examples of emotional changes may include increased nervousness, fear, grief, depression, hopelessness, helplessness, anger, irritability, feeling overwhelmed, guilt, and vulnerability.
>
> Examples of changes in thinking may include increased thinking that your future will be cut short, difficulty in remembering things, trouble making decisions, confusion, difficulty concentrating, "flashbacks" or reliving experience, nightmares, intrusive or unwelcome thoughts, too many thoughts at once, thinking about suicide, and memory gaps.

Examples of changes in behavior may include increased startle, hypervigilance, being withdrawn from others, being overly dependent upon others, changes in appetite, changes in sleep, increased substance abuse (alcohol, drugs, medication), problems with emotional or physical intimacy, inability to trust or have loving feelings, apathy, loss of spirituality, risk taking, and suicidal impulses and behaviors.

Each person may differ in the ways in which these reactions are experienced. Some may be very familiar but others may not. Many of these reactions become part of the trauma survivor's everyday life and do not seem unusual to him or her.

Each person may differ in the ways in which these reactions are experienced. Some may be very familiar but others may not. Many of these reactions become part of the trauma survivor's everyday life and do not seem unusual to him or her. Take a moment to think about the symptoms I mentioned and how many of them you experienced since the traumatic event. Are any of these symptoms familiar to you?

The question is meant to be a check-in with the client to make sure that he or she is paying attention to what the clinician is saying and understands what is being stated. The clinician should not engage in a lengthy discussion with the client about the symptoms that he or she has been experiencing.

The therapist then reads the following text to the client.

The manner in which a trauma survivor attempts to cope with his or her trauma symptoms usually has an impact on everyday activities. If a trauma survivor has recurring thoughts and memories of a trauma, he or she may attempt to avoid them by using substances (alcohol and/or drugs), becoming a workaholic, staying away from other people, and/or using anger and aggressive behavior to either distract him- or herself or remove any reminders of the trauma from the current circumstances. These strategies may give the trauma survivor short-term relief but over the long term can be problematic for a variety of reasons. In other words, sometimes a survivor's attempt to cure or to cope with reactions to a traumatic event can become a problem in and of itself.

Importantly, approaches that one might use to deal with nontraumatic events do not work very well in dealing with trauma. People will sometimes tell trauma survivors to "forget about it" and to get on with their lives. This approach may work well in many different situations, but one does not just forget about traumatic events.

One of the reasons that this advice does not work is that events that are experienced as traumatic are remembered differently from nontraumatic events. The memory of a trauma may be stored in a splintered fashion as a protection from reexperiencing the full impact of the trauma. Consequently, survivors may have amnesia for large segments of time during the trauma. Or they may remember some details of past traumas but may not have any feelings attached to these memories. They may experience overwhelming anxiety or fearfulness without understanding the cause. Certain situations may trigger flashbacks to earlier traumas, and they might feel that they are actually reliving the past.

To successfully recover from the traumatic event, it is important that you confront that experience by recounting it, repeatedly, in as much detail and with as much emotion as possible. By repeatedly recounting the event, you will be able to correct for the splintered fashion in which the memory may have been stored. You will also find that recounting the experience will result in you feeling like you have more control over the memory rather than feeling as if the memory controls you. Over the next several sessions, I will be asking you to repeatedly recount the trauma experience by writing about the experience.

After providing the client with background information about trauma and the importance of confronting it, the therapist should check to make sure that the information presented is clear to the client and to allow an opportunity for questions. The therapist then reads aloud the general writing instructions and the specific instructions for Session 1.

Over the next five sessions I would like you to write about your trauma. Don't worry about your spelling or grammar. I would like you to write about the details of the trauma as you remember it now—for example, how the trauma event happened and whether other people were involved. In writing about the details of the trauma, it is important to write about specifics of what happened and what you were feeling and thinking as the trauma was happening. Try to be as specific in recounting the details as possible. It is also important that you really let go and explore your very deepest emotions and thoughts about the trauma. You should also keep in mind that you have five sessions to write about this experience, so you don't need to be concerned with completing your account of the trauma within today's session. Just be sure to be as detailed about the trauma as possible and also to write about your thoughts and feelings as you remember them during (and immediately after) the trauma.

For your first writing session, I'd like you to write about the trauma starting at the beginning. For instance, you could begin with the moment you realized the trauma was about to happen. As you describe the trauma, it is important that you provide as many specific details as you can remember. For example, you might write about what you saw (e.g., headlights of the car approaching you, person approaching you), what you heard (e.g., car horn, screeching tires, person threatening you, explosion), or what you smelled (e.g., blood, burning rubber). In addition to writing about the details of the trauma, you should also be writing about your thoughts and feelings during the trauma as you remember it now. For example, you might have had the thought "I'm going to die," "This can't be happening," or "I'm going to be raped." And you might have felt terrified, frozen with fear, or angry at another person involved.

Remember, you don't need to finish writing about the entire trauma in this session. Just focus on writing with as much detail as possible and include the thoughts and feelings you experienced during and immediately after the trauma. Remember, the trauma is not actually happening again, you are simply recounting it as you look back upon it now.

After providing the instructions for writing, the clinician should check to make sure that the instructions are clear and that the client knows what he or she will be writing about (i.e., the specific event that will be the focus). The clinician should give the material just read to the client for reference during the writing session, if needed. Once the client confirms that the instructions are clear, the clinician should remind the client that 30 minutes are allotted to writing, that the entire 30 minutes should be used for writing, and that the clinician will keep track of the time and signal when the time is up. If the client completes the description and has the time, then he or she should start from the beginning and repeat the description. The clinician should then take a SUDS rating from the client according to how he or she feels at that moment and then signal the start of the 30 minutes of writing.

After the Writing Is Completed

After 30 minutes have elapsed, the clinician should instruct the client to stop writing. If the client is in the middle of a sentence, he or she should be allowed to finish the sentence. At this point, the clinician should take a SUDS rating of how the client is feeling at that moment.

The clinician should then check in with the client about the writing session (e.g., by asking how the session went). It is very important that this discussion is brief and focuses only on the experience of engaging in the writing (e.g., how it felt to do the writing, what was difficult or challenging about it, did the client remember more than he or she expected), rather than the details of the trauma experience or a recounting of the traumatic event. Having the client recount what he or she wrote should be avoided because the exposure has already taken place through the narrative writing. Moreover, having the client verbally recount the traumatic memory to the therapist would require substantial time and would potentially cause the client to become distressed rather than wrap up the session. As a rough guide, we suggest that this check-in should take no more than 10 minutes. If the clinician finds that it takes more than 10 minutes, then it is likely that he or she is doing more than just checking in with the client about the writing session.

If the client reports a high SUDS rating following the writing (and perhaps higher than what was reported prior to the start of the writing), the clinician should advise that it is normal to have a high rating after the first, and maybe even second, session. However, it is expected that the SUDS rating will decrease by the end of the writing sessions. If a low SUDS rating is reported, then the clinician should probe to find out why the rating was low. This could be a sign that the client was holding back and not writing a full account. For instance, the client may have written about peripheral details about the traumatic experience instead of writing about the event itself.

The clinician should not read the narrative during the session but instead wait until after the session ends and the client has left the office. We return to reading the trauma narrative when describing instructions for the second session.

After the check-in is completed, the clinician should conclude the first session using the following text.

> You will likely have thoughts, images, and feelings concerning the trauma you just wrote about during the course of the upcoming week. It is important that you allow yourself to have these thoughts, images, and feelings, whatever they might be, rather than trying to push them away. Please try to allow yourself to have whatever thoughts, images, and feelings that may come up.

The goal of this prompt is to remind the client not to avoid thoughts, images, and feelings surrounding the trauma memory.

Preparing the Client for the Possibility of Symptom Exacerbation

As described in Chapter 3, it is not uncommon to observe PTSD symptom increases during the course of WET, especially in the first few sessions. At the end of Session 1, the client should be informed that it is not unusual to not want to return for the second and maybe even third session out of a desire to avoid the trauma memory. In addition, it is not unusual for clients to experience an increase in PTSD symptoms early in the course of treatment because they are spending more time thinking about the trauma. However, clients typically find that confronting their trauma memory gets easier over the course of treatment and that the initial increase in PTSD symptoms is followed by a significant reduction in symptom severity. In fact, the increase in symptoms can be viewed as a sign that the treatment is going well because it signals that the client is engaged in the treatment and is thinking about the trauma memory. We have provided the following boxed text as an example of how to talk with clients about avoidance behaviors and analogies that can be used to illustrate the importance of confronting the trauma memory. Because the information about avoidance is not part of the WET protocol, the information is not included in the instructions that are given to clients and is not included in the Appendix.

> Avoidance is a very common symptom of PTSD that gets in the way of recovery. One way in which avoidance may come up in treatment is that people avoid coming to sessions, particularly at the beginning of a treatment when their symptoms have not yet started to decrease. Over this next week, you may have the urge to not come to our next session. It is crucial that you come to the next session. Although it is common for people to experience a symptom increase in the first couple of treatment sessions, we actually see an increase as a sign that the treatment is working because your mind is avoiding less.
>
> It is similar to (pick one of the following two analogies):
>
> *Analogy 1.* Exercising or lifting weights. If you haven't worked out in a long time, you will feel very sore at the beginning. However, if you push through this soreness and continue to regularly work out, the soreness goes away and you will start to strengthen the muscles. If you feel sore after the first workout and stop because you are sore and you did not enjoy working out,

not only do you not get stronger, but now you also made yourself suffer with soreness for a few days with no benefit. By coming to the assessment and to today's first appointment, you have done those first few workouts and your symptoms or soreness might increase as a result. Try your best to think about this as a positive sign in the way that you have seen muscle soreness as a good sign that you are working hard. Now is the time to push through the soreness so that you can get the real benefit of this treatment.

Analogy 2. Taking a medication that has side effects. Often the way medications work is that in the first few days or weeks that you start a medication, you may feel the side effects most strongly but don't really reap the benefits yet. If you stop during that time, not only will the medication not help you in the way you hoped, but now you also made yourself suffer with the side effects for a few days or weeks with no gain. By coming to the assessment and to today's first appointment, it's as if you have taken a medication for the first few days and your symptoms or side effects might increase as a result. Try your best to think about this not as a bad sign or problem—similar to how medication side effects are a good sign that you are taking the medication regularly. Now is the time to push through these symptoms so that you can get the real benefit of this treatment.

SESSION 2

Preparing for Session 2: Reviewing the Trauma Narrative

The trauma narrative from the first writing session should be read by the clinician before the start of Session 2. Several things are important to evaluate with the narrative. First, evaluate whether the client followed the writing instructions. A common deviation is that clients write about the details of an event but not their thoughts and feelings. In such instances, in the next session the clinician could tell the client that the details of the event were well written but that little mention was made about his or her thoughts and feelings. The client should be encouraged to focus on thoughts and feelings about the event in the next writing session. Another common deviation that happens in the first writing session is that clients spend most if not all of the time writing about the events that led up to the trauma instead of writing about the trauma itself. Sometimes the client will just be starting to write about the trauma when the 30 minutes are over. When this happens, the client might be highly aroused when the clinician enters the room to end the writing session and request the client's SUDS rating. This may account for why clients may report a high SUDS rating at the end of the writing. When this occurs, clients should be told that the SUDS level was understandably high because they were just starting to write about the beginning of the trauma when they were asked to stop writing. The clinician should instruct clients to start the writing (in Session 2) at the time the trauma began and then provide details as the event subsequently unfolded.

The second aspect of the trauma narrative that should be evaluated is the degree to which the client wrote about the trauma that was discussed with the clinician and remained focused in his or her writing about that event. Clients will sometimes write about a different trauma than what was agreed upon. If this happens, the clinician should ask why they wrote about a different trauma. If clients wrote about a different trauma because they realized that the event they wrote about was more upsetting and caused them more distress than the event previously discussed with the clinician, then it is okay to continue to write about this event during the remaining sessions. However, clients should be reminded that they need to stay with the same event moving forward. If a different event was selected because clients thought it would be easier or less distressing to write about, then the clinician needs to encourage them to write about the more distressing event starting with Session 2. Clients should be reminded that writing about the most distressing event leads to the best treatment outcome. They are not likely to experience much, if any, benefit if they write about a trauma that is less distressing to them. Reminding them that they are merely writing about the trauma memory rather than reliving the event is typically helpful in reducing client anxiety about confronting the trauma memory.

The third aspect of the trauma narrative that should be evaluated is the length of the account. The length will vary widely from client to client and session to session. That being said, it is typical for clients to produce written narratives that are at least several paragraphs in length at each session. If a client has only written a few sentences or one short paragraph, then the clinician should comment about how short the narrative is and ask the client for an explanation. In listening to the client's response, the clinician should assess whether the client is not writing much because he or she is trying to avoid thinking about the trauma. If this seems likely, the clinician should restate the rationale for repeatedly confronting the trauma memory and explain that such repeated confrontation is necessary for symptom reduction. If the pattern of avoidance continues into Sessions 2 and 3, then the clinician should have a frank discussion with the client about whether it makes sense to continue with the WET protocol. There is no sense in continuing with any treatment protocol when the client is not willing or able to adhere to it. It is better to discontinue a treatment in such instances rather than have the client end the protocol after five sessions with the impression that the treatment does not work.

Conducting Session 2

The instructions for Session 2 should be printed out prior to conducting the session. At the start of this session, the clinician should ask the client how things have gone since the last session. The clinician asks this question to assess how much time the client spent thinking about the trauma. The clinician also should ask the client whether he or she was able to think about the trauma rather than try to push the thoughts away.

At this point the clinician should provide the client with feedback regarding the first trauma narrative. It is important that the feedback include positive comments in addition to comments about how the narrative writing could be improved. Typically, there are some ways in which the client could improve upon how he or she wrote about the trauma during the first session, as discussed previously. After providing the feedback, the clinician should read verbatim the following instructions for Session 2 writing.

> Today, I want you to continue to write about the trauma as you look back upon it now. If you feel that you didn't get the chance to completely describe the trauma in the last writing session, then you can pick up where you left off. If you completed writing about the trauma event in the last session, please write about the entire trauma again. While you are describing the trauma, I really want you to delve into your very deepest feelings (e.g., fear, shock, sadness, anger) and thoughts (e.g., "Is this really happening?" "I'm going to die"). Also, remember to write about the details of the trauma. That is, describe the setting; the people involved; and what you saw, heard, and felt. Remember that you are writing about the trauma as you look back upon it now.

The clinician should ask the client if the instructions are clear and then ask for a SUDS rating for the client's distress at that moment. The client should be reminded that the clinician will be keeping track of time and will instruct the client when to stop writing. After conveying these instructions, the clinician should prompt the client to begin writing.

After the Writing Is Completed

After 30 minutes have elapsed, the clinician should alert the client that the time is up and to stop writing. As with the first session, the client should be allowed to complete a sentence before stopping.

At this point, the clinician should ask the client to provide a SUDS rating of his or her distress at that moment. Next, the clinician should ask the client about the writing experience during that session. If the client does not have much to say, then the clinician should ask probing questions (e.g., whether the writing session was easier in the second session than the first, whether time seemed to move quickly or slowly, or whether the client remembered more details in this session than the last session). The clinician should also inquire about how well clients attended to the feedback from the prior trauma narrative. For instance, if the client was given specific feedback to focus on thoughts and feelings because they were not incorporated into the writing during the prior session, the clinician should inquire whether they were included in this narrative.

At the conclusion of the check-in, the clinician should collect the narrative from the client, schedule the next session, and then conclude the session by stating the following text.

> As I stated at the end of the first session, you will likely have thoughts, feelings, and visual images concerning the trauma during the course of the upcoming week. It is important that you allow yourself to have these thoughts, images, and feelings, whatever they might be, rather than trying to push them away. Please try to allow yourself to have whatever thoughts, images, and feelings that come up.

SESSION 3

Preparing for Session 3

Preparation for Session 3 is the same as for Session 2. The clinician should read the trauma narrative prior to Session 3 to evaluate how well the client followed the instructions. Any issues that arose in the first session that the client was given feedback to correct in the second session should also be evaluated. If some correction has occurred but further improvement is still needed, then the client should be provided with additional feedback. For instance, if the client wrote about thoughts and feelings in the second session but only a handful of times, the clinician should acknowledge that the client did include his or her thoughts and feelings but that more of that is needed.

Conducting Session 3

An important difference in the instructions for Session 3 from Sessions 1 and 2 is that in Session 3, the client is asked to write about the impact of the trauma in addition to continuing to write a description of the trauma. However, if the client did not write a detailed trauma account in the first two sessions, instructions for Session 3 should be altered; the client should be asked to write a detailed account of the trauma with a focus on the thoughts and feelings experienced as the trauma was happening. In other words, a client who has not done an adequate job following instructions for Sessions 1 and 2 should not be asked in Session 3 to write about the impact that the event has had on his or her life.

As with the prior session, the therapist should begin the session by asking the client how he or she has been doing since the preceding session. This is a general check-in with the client that should not require more than a few minutes to conduct. The clinician should then provide feedback on the client's narrative from the last session. The following instructions for the third session are then read to the client.

> I want you to continue writing about the trauma event as you think about it today. If you have completed writing about the entire trauma you experienced, you can either write about the trauma again from the beginning or you can select a part of the trauma that is most upsetting to you and focus your writing on that specific part of the experience. In addition, I would also like you to begin to write about how the traumatic experience has changed your life. For instance, you might write about whether or not the trauma has changed the way you view your life, the meaning of life, and how you relate to other people. Throughout your writing, I want you to really let go and write about your deepest thoughts and feelings.

After reading these instructions to the client, the clinician should ask whether there are any questions about the instructions for this session. The clinician should again remind the client that he or she will have 30 minutes to write and that the clinician will keep track of time and announce when

30 minutes have elapsed. The client should be asked for a SUDS rating and then be prompted to begin writing.

After the Writing Is Completed

After 30 minutes have elapsed, the client should be prompted to stop writing. The clinician should take a SUDS rating of the client's feeling at that moment. By this time in the treatment protocol, clients should be experiencing a decrease in SUDS ratings. If that is the case, then the clinician should point out the decrease to the client. If the SUDS rating is not decreasing much yet, then the clinician should consider repeating Session 3. The clinician should also explore possible hypotheses for the lack of progress (e.g., avoidance manifested as the client not following writing instructions).

Following the SUDS rating, the clinician should ask the client how the writing session went. By this point in the WET protocol, we typically find that the after writing check-in takes less time than it did in the first two sessions, especially if the client is fully engaged in the treatment, follows the instructions, and is not avoiding thoughts and feelings about the trauma event between sessions. After the check-in is completed, the clinician should collect the narrative. The clinician should conclude Session 3 by stating the following text.

> As I've stated previously, you will likely have thoughts, feelings, and visual images concerning the trauma during the course of the upcoming week. It is important that you allow yourself to have these thoughts, images, and feelings, whatever they might be, rather than trying to push them away. Please try to allow yourself to have whatever thoughts, images, and feelings that come up.

SESSION 4

Preparing for Session 4

At this point in the treatment, the clinician should have the routine for preparing for WET sessions in place. As with prior sessions, the narrative from the prior session should be reviewed in advance of Session 4 to make sure that the instructions were followed. As previously stated for Session 3, if the client has not consistently followed the writing instructions by this point in the treatment, then the treatment will not be successful, and the clinician should talk about terminating the sessions. However, if the client is generally following instructions but is perhaps not writing as much about his or her thoughts and feelings, then the treatment sessions should proceed. Assuming the treatment moves forward, the instructions should be printed out in advance of the session so that the clinician can read them and then leave them with the client during the writing of the narrative for this session.

Conducting Session 4

At the start of the session, the clinician should again ask the client how the week went since the last session. At this time in the treatment, we often observe that clients begin to report confronting previously avoided places or activities. For example, clients who had been avoiding restaurants might report going out to dinner with a loved one since the last session. After talking with the client about the time since the last session, feedback should be given to the client regarding the trauma narrative for Session 3. At this point in the treatment, most clients are very much on track with following the instructions, and the clinician should simply state that the client did a great job following the instructions for the last session. The clinician should then provide the following instructions for Session 4.

> I want you to continue to write about the trauma today. As with your writing in the last session, you can select a specific part of the trauma to write about; that is, the part of the trauma that was most upsetting to you. Today, I would also like you to write about how the trauma event has changed your life. You might write about whether the trauma has changed the way you view your life, the meaning of life, and how you relate to other people. Throughout the session I want you to really let go and write about your deepest thoughts and feelings.

After giving these instructions, the clinician should ask whether the client has any questions about the instructions for the session. The clinician should again remind the client that he or she has 30 minutes to write and that the clinician will keep track of time and announce when to stop writing. The client should be asked for a SUDS rating right before the prompt is given to begin writing.

After the Writing Is Completed

After 30 minutes have elapsed, the client should be prompted to stop writing. The clinician should ask for a SUDS rating of the client's feelings at that moment; the decreases in SUDS ratings should continue. If that is the case, then the clinician should point this out to the client. If SUDS ratings are not yet decreasing appreciably, then there should be some exploration of possible reasons. As in the prior session, the clinician should explore possible hypotheses for the lack of progress.

Following the SUDS rating, the clinician should ask the client about the writing session. As with the prior session, we typically find this discussion to be fairly brief by this phase of the treatment. After the check-in is completed, the narrative should be collected by the clinician and the following text should be stated verbatim to end the session.

> As I've stated previously, you will likely have thoughts, feelings, and visual images concerning the trauma during the course of this week. It is important that you allow yourself to have these thoughts, images, and feelings, whatever they might be, rather than trying to push them away. Please try to allow yourself to have whatever thoughts, images, and feelings that come up.

The clinician should remind the client that the next session will be the final writing session.

SESSION 5

Preparing for Session 5

This is the last session of the treatment protocol. The narrative from the prior session should be reviewed to provide feedback to the client. However, there is typically no feedback given at this point in the treatment. Note that the instructions for the last session differ from the prior sessions in that the client is asked to "wrap-up" the writing by describing how he or she plans to move forward. The instructions for Session 5 should be printed out and read to the client. As with all sessions, the printout of the instructions should be given to the client.

Conducting Session 5

At the start of the session, the clinician should again ask the client about the interval since the last session. We generally provide positive feedback regarding the last narrative, because clients are typically following the instructions and fully engaged in the narrative at this point in the treatment. The clinician should then remind the client that this is the final session of writing and then proceed with reading the following instructions for the session.

> Today is the last session. I want you to continue to write about your feelings and thoughts related to the traumatic event and how you believe this event has changed your life. Remember that this is the last day of writing and so you might want to try to wrap up your writing. For example, you might write about how the traumatic experience is related to your current life and your future. As with the other writing sessions, it is important for you to delve into your deepest emotions and thoughts throughout the session.

After the instructions are given, the clinician should ask whether there are any questions and again remind the client that the writing time is 30 minutes and that the clinician will keep track of time and announce when to stop writing. The client should be asked for a SUDS rating of his or her feelings at that moment and then be prompted to begin writing.

After the Writing Is Completed

Once 30 minutes have elapsed, the client should be prompted to stop writing. The clinician should take a SUDS rating from the client and then ask about the writing session. Given that this is the final session, the clinician should inquire more generally about whether the client believes the treatment has been beneficial and whether he or she believes that additional treatment is needed. The client should be reminded that he or she has learned how to cope with a traumatic experience so that if PTSD symptoms develop in the future, the client has learned a skill that can be used to cope with those symptoms. The clinician should also point out that all of the instructions throughout the course of the treatment have been given to the client for future reference.

If the client believes that he or she is still experiencing residual PTSD symptoms, then several options should be discussed. One option is to continue to conduct WET. The client may benefit from doing the writing sessions again with another trauma event or might feel that the five sessions were not long enough to address the trauma event that was the focus of treatment. This scenario is most likely to happen when someone was not following instructions (writing about peripheral details of the event rather than directly writing about the event, switching between trauma events) in the first session or two of the treatment. A second option would be to use a different evidence-based treatment for PTSD. Prolonged exposure also has a primary focus on imaginal exposure; cognitive processing therapy might be a good second treatment option following WET because it is primarily a cognitive treatment that addresses trauma-related cognitions.

Alternatively, some clients will complete WET reporting that they have experienced reductions in many PTSD symptoms but that they have other symptoms that require treatment, such as depression, substance use, or emotion dysregulation. In such cases, evidence-based treatments that are most appropriate for those presenting problems should be considered.

5 FREQUENTLY ASKED QUESTIONS ABOUT DELIVERING WRITTEN EXPOSURE THERAPY

Over the course of our experience with training others on the written exposure therapy (WET) protocol, a number of questions from clinicians have
been raised. Below is a list of those recurring questions and our responses
to them. Most of the scenarios that are the focus of these questions are not
common, but they may occur from time to time during the delivery of WET
and many evidence-based treatments for PTSD. Some of the questions have
already been addressed, but we include them in this chapter to provide a
comprehensive list of questions that clinicians frequently ask.

What if clients express concern about their writing ability or the readability of their handwriting?

When clients express concern about writing because they believe they are
not very good writers, it should be emphasized that the quality of the writing
does not matter. The goal of the writing is to confront the trauma memory;
grammar, sentence structure, and spelling are not important. Clients should
be assured that they will not be judged on the quality of their narrative. Clients
who express concern about the legibility of their handwriting should again be
reassured that this aspect of the writing does not matter. The therapist will

http://dx.doi.org/10.1037/0000139-006
Written Exposure Therapy for PTSD: A Brief Treatment Approach for Mental Health Professionals, by D. M. Sloan and B. P. Marx

need to be able to read the text to make sure that the instructions have been followed but can always check with the client to clarify what is written if the handwriting is hard to decipher.

How do you handle clients who have a physical condition that prevents them from writing?

There are times when it is not possible for clients to write because of a hand injury or a significant visual impairment (e.g., legally blind). For clients who cannot write by hand, we have provided a digital recorder to talk into instead of writing. We have found that this procedure works well for such situations. We have not used this method when clients voice concerns about the legibility of their handwriting or general concern about handwriting (as opposed to typing). For instance, some clients might state that they would be more comfortable typing the trauma narrative rather than writing by hand. As stated in a prior chapter, we have found the method of writing by hand to be optimal because it slows down the process of recounting the event, permitting the client to recall more details, thoughts, and feelings of the event. Typing the narrative can be problematic; good typists are likely to move too quickly through the imaginal exposure. On the other hand, clients who are not good typists might experience cognitive distraction through the process of typing.

What if clients stop writing before the end of the 30 minutes?

If clients come out of the room before 30 minutes have passed and tell you they are done, you should gently ask them to go back in the room, sit down, and start writing again from the beginning, remembering to follow the instructions that were given. Similarly, if clients tell you that they stopped writing and just sat in the room until you returned, you should remind them that they should start from the beginning again and keep writing until you return and tell them to stop. When clients stop writing before the 30 minutes have passed, the narrative typically lacks sufficient detail; when this happens, you should provide such feedback to them before the start of the next writing session.

What if clients claim that they wrote for the entire 30 minutes but their narrative is very brief?

If the narrative is very brief, then there is a good chance that they did not write for the full 30 minutes. In such cases, you should tell them that the narrative is short and ask whether they wrote the entire time. If clients maintain that they did indeed write for the entire 30 minutes, then you should reiterate the importance of writing for the full 30 minutes in order to gain benefits from the treatment. Encourage clients to provide more details during the next session to enhance the possibility of benefiting from the treatment.

What if clients have multiple traumas (e.g., combat exposure or childhood abuse) and, as a result, are unable to choose one specific event about which to write?

This is not an uncommon situation, especially when clients have experienced chronic traumatic events, such as child abuse. In such cases, you should ask whether any one event really stands out. If there are none or if the they are unable to choose between more than one, then they should be told to select the event for which they have a good memory and can write about with a lot of details. If there are several such events, then clients should be instructed to pick one event and focus on it. It is important to write about that same event repeatedly over the course of all the writing sessions and not switch between different events even if they are equally traumatic.

What if someone states at the beginning of the first writing session that he or she has writer's block and can't write about the traumatic event?

In our experience this rarely happens, although clients might think that writing about the event will be difficult. Clinicians should express understanding that writing about the event may be difficult but also express confidence that people generally are able to write about their events after they get started. It's also important to remind them that, in all likelihood, they think about the event all the time but that writing about it will likely feel different because they are controlling the memory instead of the memory occurring in an intrusive way.

Limit the amount of time you spend discussing clients' reluctance about writing, because it may serve as a way to avoid starting to write; the more time they spend thinking about the task, the more likely they are to want to avoid doing it. Clients should be encouraged to do the best that they can and to be reminded that you will be back in 30 minutes to tell them to stop writing.

What if clients write for 30 minutes but do not report any arousal or distress during the writing sessions?

At the end of the session, carefully review the narrative to make sure that they followed the instructions and wrote details of the event itself (and not details leading up to or following the event). Another possibility is that clients may not be writing about the event most closely connected with the PTSD symptoms, because they do not want to confront the intense feelings associated with that event. This possibility is explored in Case 2 in the next chapter.

What if clients change the writing topic midway through the treatment without discussing this with you?

Changing the topic of the writing sessions may be a form of avoidance and should not be permitted. It is crucial that clients write about the same event during each session because the treatment is based on an exposure model; repeated exposure to the same stimulus (i.e., trauma memory) is necessary to receive therapeutic benefits. When clients select and write about a specific event during the first writing session, they should continue to write about that same event during the remainder of the sessions.

What if clients don't notice any immediate symptom relief?

If clients report that they have not noticed any changes in symptoms, reassure them that this is normal and that they may not experience any relief until all the writing sessions are completed. Similarly, if clients report an increase in their symptoms, reassure them that it's not uncommon to experience an increase in symptoms before seeing a decrease. In fact, a brief, temporary symptom increase may be a good sign, because it signals that they are engaged in the writing. As long as they do not avoid any future writing sessions (or reminders of the trauma either during or outside of therapy) and continue to be engaged, the symptoms will subside. In general, an increase in symptoms, especially early in the course of sessions, is a positive prognostic sign.

What if clients can't focus or can't follow instructions even after repeated direct feedback?

In such situations, you should ask them what is getting in the way of their focus. Staying in the room with clients during the writing may improve their focus. If they aren't following directions, even after repeated redirection, it may be that they are unwilling to follow the instructions. In a few rare instances that we are aware of, clients were not willing to engage in the writing exercises despite the best attempts by the therapist. In such cases, it is best to have an open and honest conversation about their commitment to therapy.

What if clients do not want to share their writing with the clinician?

We have used WET with hundreds of individuals and not a single client has withheld his or her narrative from the therapist. In fact, we find that people want to share their narratives with the therapist. We have treated several people who wanted copies of their narratives after they completed their writing, and we have gladly complied with that request. Nonetheless, if someone indicates that he or she does not want to give the written narrative to the therapist, you should respect those wishes. However, the client must let the therapist read the narrative, so that he or she can provide feedback in subsequent sessions. When clients voice strong objections to sharing the narrative, the reason for their objection should be discussed.

What if clients maintain that they are not capable of expressing themselves in writing?

It's not the quality of writing that leads to beneficial outcomes, but rather the act of confronting the trauma event through writing. We have treated clients who had a 3rd grade education who completed WET and benefited from it. If clients express concern that they aren't good writers or don't think they can do a good job with the writing, you should reassure them that grammar, spelling, and writing structure are not important. If they are not physically capable of writing (e.g., have a disability or injury), you can provide a digital recorder and have them verbalize the narrative instead of writing it out.

What if clients decide to discontinue the writing after the first or second session?

WET is a very well-tolerated treatment. Premature treatment dropout rates have been very low in all studies (e.g., 5%–10%). However, in the event that clients wish to prematurely terminate treatment, you should try to convince them to complete additional sessions. Ask them for their reason for wanting to drop out. If they report that they have been experiencing an increase in PTSD symptoms since they started writing (which can sometimes present as anger about the writing sessions or objections to repeatedly writing about the event), you should reassure them that this is not uncommon, especially in the first couple of sessions, and that symptoms will diminish if they persist with the writing. In fact, the worst thing they could do under those conditions is to stop treatment at the point that they are having an increase in symptoms; this will only reinforce the notion that the trauma, and reminders of it, should be avoided.

What if clients state that they are reluctant to complete the treatment because they are concerned it will make them think too much about the trauma memory?

Client concerns about thinking too much about the trauma are not unusual in trauma-focused treatment. Paradoxically, individuals with PTSD think about their trauma all the time but they do so in an uncontrolled and intrusive manner. The clinician should point this out and let them know that trauma-focused treatment provides an opportunity to have better control of their trauma memories by allowing them to think about them rather than attempting to push the thoughts away. The result of confronting trauma memories is that the memories will not be as distressing. It is also important to remind clients that they are merely remembering the trauma event, not reliving it.

What if clients feel the need to talk about the trauma in-depth with the clinician (i.e., won't stop talking before or after writing)?

Keep the session focused on the writing. Politely let them know that it's important to get started on the writing (if they want to talk before they begin writing). If they persist in talking about the writing or other topics after the writing and debriefing have been completed, politely tell them that you need to wrap up the session but that you can continue to discuss their reactions to the writing the next time they come in for a writing session.

What if English is not the client's primary language?

WET can be used as long as clients are able to read and write in English. Of course, if the therapist is able to understand the client's primary language (e.g., Spanish), then it would be best to use that language.

What if clients dissociate during the writing?

Very rarely has anyone dissociated during a writing session. However, when this has happened we offer to stay in the room during the next writing session as a way to keep them grounded. We also offer grounding techniques (e.g., grabbing tightly onto one's chair, digging heels into the floor). If you stay in the room during the writing, be sure to let clients know that you will not be interacting with them during the writing. The sole purpose of staying in the room is to decrease the likelihood of client dissociation during the session. In the next chapter, we present a case example of a client who dissociated during WET to illustrate how this situation was managed.

What if clients want to shift the focus of the session to discuss ongoing life stressors they are experiencing?

Individuals diagnosed with PTSD frequently have a number of ongoing life stressors, including employment, financial, and relationship issues. It is not uncommon for clients to present to a given session wanting to focus on their ongoing life stressors rather than focus on WET. In such situations, it is best to continue to conduct the WET sessions rather than provide general support for chronic stressors. It is helpful to remind clients that the clinician can best serve them by treating the PTSD symptoms, which, in turn, will enable them to better manage their life stressors. Appropriate referrals for ongoing stressors, such as housing or financial issues, can be made, but the focus should remain on conducting WET.

6

CASE ILLUSTRATIONS

In this chapter, we present several case examples of individuals treated with written exposure therapy (WET) to illustrate how to manage common scenarios that might arise when implementing WET with clients. The cases in this chapter are composites of clients we have treated; to protect their identity, we have altered their names and demographic information.

CASE 1: HISTORY OF MULTIPLE TRAUMA EVENTS

It is quite common for individuals with posttraumatic stress disorder (PTSD) to have been exposed to more than one potentially traumatic experience or have an index event consisting of repeated traumatic events, such as childhood sexual or physical abuse, combat trauma, or domestic violence (De Jongh et al., 2016), and to have been diagnosed with a personality disorder, such as borderline personality disorder (Harned, Rizvi, & Linehan, 2010). Although some clinicians may believe that it would not be appropriate to use WET with clients with such trauma histories and symptom profiles, we have a successful track record of treating such individuals.

http://dx.doi.org/10.1037/0000139-007
Written Exposure Therapy for PTSD: A Brief Treatment Approach for Mental Health Professionals, by D. M. Sloan and B. P. Marx

Robert was a single, White male military veteran in his 50s presenting for treatment of PTSD related to childhood physical abuse. Robert had multiple psychiatric diagnoses including PTSD, major depression, borderline personality disorder, and alcohol dependence in remission. He also had an extensive treatment history that included a full course of cognitive processing therapy, a partial course of prolonged exposure therapy, two admissions to a residential substance abuse treatment (minimum stay 30 days), at least one course of outpatient treatment for his depression, and several courses of an outpatient therapy skills group. Typically, Robert would drop out of these therapy groups because he had difficulties getting along with other group members and following the group rules (e.g., consistent attendance). Robert frequently had numerous ongoing life stressors (e.g., interpersonal stressors, work stressors) that interfered with treatment for his psychiatric conditions.

We present this case to illustrate how to choose a specific trauma as a focus for the written narratives when the client has multiple events from which to choose, how to manage chronic life stressors in the context of PTSD treatment, and how to use WET to effectively treat someone who presents with emotion regulation difficulties in combination with a prior PTSD treatment history.

Robert's initial session with his therapist was spent discussing therapy goals, assessing PTSD symptoms, and deciding on the treatment plan. Robert scored a 56 on the PTSD Checklist for the *Diagnostic and Statistical Manual of Mental Disorders, Fifth Edition* (PCL-5; Weathers, Litz, et al., 2013), indicating a probable PTSD diagnosis and high PTSD symptom severity. The therapist and Robert agreed to a course of WET, given that he previously received unsuccessful courses of cognitive processing therapy and prolonged exposure therapy. Robert also liked the idea of conducting written narratives in the clinic rather than at home, and he indicated that he also thought writing about the event would be more helpful than recounting the event out loud to the therapist. The next session was scheduled with the understanding that they would be starting WET at that time.

The first session started with the therapist asking Robert to identify a specific episode of childhood abuse that would be the focus of the writing. This was challenging since the abuse Robert experienced occurred over 6 years and included numerous abusive episodes. Robert stated that he had difficulty selecting one event because he felt that doing so would discount the importance of his other trauma experiences. The therapist clarified that selecting one event did not mean that the other events were not important but that focusing on one especially upsetting event in the writing would provide an opportunity to look at it from a different perspective. Moreover, he was told that he had the option to focus on other experiences in additional writing sessions after the initial five sessions were completed. This information seemed to comfort Robert. Although he was able to subsequently identify three events that were most upsetting to him (e.g., the subjects of frequently intrusive thoughts and nightmares), he was unable to choose one event on which he would begin his writing. The therapist asked Robert if his memory was better for one of the events than the others. He stated that his memory was particularly strong for two of the three events and that one of these two events represented a more frequent abuse scenario that he had experienced. Based on this information, the therapist and Robert decided that he would focus on the event for which he had a strong memory and that represented a frequently experienced scenario.

The therapist explained that WET is a structured treatment, that most of it is scripted, and that instructions would be read aloud to Robert. The therapist read information regarding the treatment rationale to Robert, who readily understood and was eager to get started. The therapist asked Robert to provide a rating of his discomfort, as measured by the Subjective Units of Distress Scale (SUDS; Wolpe, 1958) according to how he was feeling at that moment. Robert provided a SUDS rating of 70, indicating relatively strong distress and apprehension. The therapist then read the Session 1 writing instructions to Robert, made sure that he understood what he was supposed to do, and then left him to write. Upon completing the writing, the therapist again asked Robert to provide a SUDS rating. He reported a rating of 85. (Such an increase in SUDS is common during the first exposure session for clients who engage in trauma-focused treatments such as WET. This should not be cause for immediate concern, because it is an indication that the client is engaged and fully participating. Clients should be told to expect such increases and, should they occur, not to be deterred from continuing with the treatment.) The therapist then asked Robert how the writing session went for him. Robert indicated that he wrote for the full 30 minutes and was surprised how fast the time had gone by. He asked if he could continue to write for another 10 to 20 minutes. The therapist explained that the sessions were structured such that only 30 minutes of writing were allotted per session and that if he did not finish his writing in the first session, there would be plenty of time to do so in the upcoming sessions. The therapist collected Robert's written narrative and restated that she would be reading it before the next session to make sure that he followed directions. The therapist asked Robert to provide another SUDS rating for how he was feeling at that point, after their conversation. He gave a rating of 60, indicating that the high level of distress he had felt immediately following the writing had decreased. The therapist instructed Robert that if he found himself having thoughts, images, or feelings about the trauma about which he wrote during the course of the week, he should allow himself to experience them, whatever they might be, rather than push them away. Robert agreed to "try his best" not to avoid thoughts, images, and feelings. The next session was then scheduled and Session 1 ended.

Robert presented for the second WET session 1 week later. At the beginning of this session, Robert told the therapist that he had a difficult week due to a verbal argument with his neighbor, among other things. He stated that he wanted to spend the session discussing the past week. The therapist told Robert that, although she appreciated he had a challenging week, they needed to stay focused on the trauma that Robert identified in Session 1 because the goal of their work together was to conduct the trauma-focused treatment. The therapist advised him that by addressing his PTSD symptoms, he would be better able to manage the interpersonal difficulties in his life that he reported were a frequent occurrence. Although disappointed, Robert stated that he understood the treatment goal and agreed to continue with the second WET session. The therapist then provided Robert with feedback about his first writing session. In general, Robert had followed the instructions by providing a detailed account of his trauma, including some thoughts and emotions he had about the trauma. However, the therapist encouraged Robert to write more fully about the emotions he experienced during the incident. The therapist gave the instructions for the second writing session to Robert and then asked for his SUDS rating, which he reported as 65. Robert was then prompted to start the writing once the therapist left the room.

After the 30 minutes of writing, the therapist returned and asked for Robert's SUDS rating. Robert reported a SUDS rating of 60. The therapist noted the decrease in SUDS from the prior session; Robert noted that the second session seemed easier than the first session. Robert also stated that he was finding writing about the trauma very helpful in terms of sorting out the sequence of the traumatic event he experienced as well as providing him with an "outlet" to confront the emotions he had about his traumatic experience. Robert indicated that although writing about this event was upsetting, it was more tolerable than he anticipated it would be. The therapist scheduled the next session with Robert and then instructed him to not avoid thoughts, images, or feelings about the traumatic event during the course of the upcoming week.

The remaining three sessions progressed well. Specifically, Robert followed the writing instructions for each trauma narrative and reported feeling increasingly less distressed about the trauma memory. This reduction in his distress was also noted in progressively decreased SUDS ratings from session to session. In addition to the reduction in his distress level, his PTSD symptom severity decreased by 30 points from baseline to the last WET session (baseline PCL-5 score = 54; last WET session PCL score = 24). Moreover, his post-treatment score was indicative of no longer meeting PTSD diagnostic criteria.

During the last session, Robert reported that he found WET to be very beneficial as the treatment allowed him to "work through" his trauma and make sense of what happened to him. He also reported that he had not had this experience with other trauma-focused treatments.

In supervision, the therapist noted to the supervisor that she was surprised how smoothly the treatment had gone with Robert, who had a history of having difficulty in treatment as a result of emotional dysregulation manifested as binge drinking, cutting behavior, and angry outbursts during the sessions. None of these behaviors were displayed during the WET sessions; he remained focused despite numerous life stressors during the course of treatment that would have distracted him in the past. Moreover, Robert consistently attended the WET sessions, unlike his attendance during previous treatment efforts. It was the therapist's perception that the highly structured nature of the treatment, in combination with the limited therapist interaction during the exposures, enabled Robert to remain focused throughout the treatment. Following the five WET sessions, Robert and the therapist agreed that he no longer needed treatment for his PTSD. Robert did present to the clinic several months later and was referred for dialectical behavior therapy for ongoing difficulties with emotion regulation.

CASE 2: INDEX TRAUMA NOT DISCLOSED UNTIL LATER IN TREATMENT

Sometimes clients do not initially disclose the event associated with their PTSD symptoms because they wish to avoid the intense distress, shame, or guilt they feel when they think about such experiences. In such cases, they may report other experiences that don't cause them as much distress or discomfort. However, after the client becomes more comfortable with the therapist, he or she may later disclose the actual traumatic event that causes the most difficulties. Alternatively, the therapist may suspect that the client did not provide the correct index event at the outset of treatment, either because the client's SUDS ratings never attained levels that indicate that he or she is writing about the event that is most strongly connected with his or her symptoms, or because the client seems to be keeping important details from the written narratives. For example, a combat veteran might generally report a combat event as his most distressing experience, but because his SUDS do not elevate sufficiently during the initial writing sessions, the therapist suspects that the client has not disclosed substantial details and discusses that possibility with him. Only then does the client report that the experience that causes him the most distress is an event in which he shot a child during his combat deployment. Should such a situation occur, the focus of treatment should shift accordingly and sessions already completed may need to be readministered to achieve treatment benefit. This very scenario happened with one of our clients, referred to here as Wendy. She initially reported another index event that did not cause her substantial distress and did not disclose the trauma related to her PTSD symptoms until later in the treatment.

Wendy was a single, African American woman in her early 40s who presented for treatment of PTSD symptoms related to a robbery at knifepoint 10 years prior. Wendy indicated that she was not physically harmed in the robbery and the assailant fled the scene as soon as she handed him her purse. Nonetheless, she reportedly experienced significant PTSD symptoms immediately following this event and stated that these symptoms caused her significant social and occupational impairment. She had not received prior PTSD treatment but had received approximately eight sessions of supportive counseling following the robbery. She reported a mild decrease in her symptoms following these sessions, but this reduction was short-lived. Aside from the robbery, Wendy noted that she had not experienced any other traumatic life event. Upon presentation to the clinic, Wendy completed the PCL-5 to assess her PTSD symptom severity. She received a score of 49, indicating probable PTSD diagnosis and severe PTSD symptom severity. Several PTSD treatment options were presented to Wendy; she chose WET because she believed this would be a good approach for her. The therapist and Wendy scheduled a session to begin therapy.

Wendy presented to the first therapy session eager to start the treatment. She used the entire 30 minutes allotted for the writing. Notably, her SUDS rating prior to the writing was 30 and only increased to 35 following the writing session. The therapist also noted that Wendy did not seem very distressed by the writing session. When asked about her mild SUDS rating, Wendy indicated that she was engaged in the writing session but she did not feel very distressed while writing about the experience. Noting that her SUDS might be low because of the way she wrote about the event, the therapist stated that she would be reading the narrative and providing Wendy with feedback at the next session, which was scheduled for the following week.

At the second WET session the therapist told Wendy that she had read the trauma narrative and was surprised that Wendy's SUDS rating was relatively low, given how detailed the narrative was about the event as well as her thoughts and feelings surrounding the event. The therapist then asked Wendy if her SUDS had increased during the writing session but then decreased by the end of the session. Wendy reported that she was unsure but thought that pattern might have occurred. The therapist then presented the instructions for the second session to Wendy, and she proceeded with the writing. Similar to the first session, Wendy reported relatively low SUDS prior to the writing session with just a 5-point increase reported at the end of the session. The therapist again asked Wendy if her SUDS rating was higher during the course of the writing; Wendy stated that she believed that was the case. Following the session, the therapist read the narrative and noted that it was consistent in detail and length as the narrative Wendy produced in the first session.

A similar pattern was noted during the third session. In addition, the weekly PCL-5 that Wendy completed indicated that she not only continued to experience very high levels of PTSD symptoms, but her score of 54 was slightly higher than her baseline score of 49. When the therapist noted the lack of PTSD symptom reduction to Wendy, she agreed that her symptoms remained high even though she felt the sessions were helpful in confronting her trauma memory. The therapist raised the possibility to Wendy that, should things not change, they might consider trying a different therapy approach. Wendy indicated a strong preference to continue with the WET sessions because she believed the treatment was helpful, and the therapist agreed to proceed with WET.

Wendy presented to the fourth WET session the following week, stating that there was something she needed to talk about with the therapist. Wendy disclosed that the robbery incident that she previously identified as the index event for her PTSD symptoms was, in fact, not related to her current PTSD symptoms. Instead, her symptoms were related to a prior sexual assault. Wendy stated that she felt shame about this incident and did not feel comfortable talking about it with the therapist when she initially presented to treatment. Wendy also disclosed that given the focus of the treatment, she understood that she would not benefit from treatment unless she confided in the therapist about the sexual assault. The therapist thanked Wendy for her honesty and told her she understood her reluctance to disclose the assault. The therapist also let Wendy know that the severity of her symptoms were surprising to her given the robbery incident that she had described but that her symptom presentation fit better with someone who was sexually assaulted. Now that the event driving the PTSD symptoms was known, they could focus the treatment accordingly.

The therapist suggested to Wendy that they should start over with the WET sessions to focus on the sexual assault. Wendy agreed to this plan. The therapist then presented the writing instructions for the first session (without presenting the PTSD psychoeducation information and therapy rationale). Wendy then proceeded to write for the allotted 30 minutes. Not unexpectedly, Wendy reported an initial SUDS rating of 60 prior to writing that increased to 80 by the end of the session. Unlike the prior sessions, Wendy was visibly upset following the writing session. She was tearful and reported that it was difficult to write about the assault, especially given how much she usually avoided thinking about this event. An examination of the trauma narrative indicated that Wendy had followed the instructions for the writing with the exception of not writing about the emotions related to the sexual assault.

The second WET session that focused on the sexual assault proceeded well. Wendy responded to the feedback to write about the emotions she experienced in addition to writing about the details and her thoughts about the event. Her SUDS remained relatively high but were slightly lower than the prior session. Her SUDS ratings progressively decreased over the course of the next three writing sessions. Wendy also reported that she experienced few or no PTSD symptoms and that for the first time since the assault she no longer had a sense of shame or responsibility for the event. The PCL completed during the last WET session indicated a substantial decrease from baseline, with a score of 15 at posttreatment, which is indicative of no longer meeting PTSD diagnostic criteria. As a result of these treatment gains, Wendy decided that she did not need any additional treatment sessions. The therapist concurred, and treatment was ended.

CASE 3: PHYSICAL LIMITATIONS THAT PREVENT WRITING

Some clients present with physical limitations that may preclude writing. This next case illustrates how WET can still be used when physical limitations prevent a client from engaging in writing. When Matthew began WET, he was able to write, but after completing two sessions he suffered an accident in which he broke his right wrist; he was unable to write during the final sessions. Drawing on research showing that emotional expression works similarly through writing or speaking into an audio recorder (Smyth & Pennebaker, 2016), we shifted our approach to using a digital recorder for the remaining treatment sessions.

Matthew was a divorced White male in his 60s who presented for treatment of chronic PTSD symptoms related to witnessing a woman being struck and killed by a car 20 years earlier. He reported that not only did he witness the accident, but he also went to the aid of woman after she was struck and that she died in his arms while they waited for an ambulance to arrive.

Matthew noted that he used his work as an accountant to distract himself from thoughts about the accident but now that he was retired he found himself unable to effectively cope with intrusive thoughts about the event. He initially sought psychotherapy following the accident but he reported that this therapy was support-oriented and did not provide him with any notable symptom relief. He stopped attending this treatment after seven sessions because he was not receiving any benefits from it. At baseline, the therapist administered the PCL-5 to assess his PTSD symptom severity. His score on the PCL-5 was 46, indicating probable PTSD diagnosis and severe PTSD symptoms. The therapist presented Matthew with several PTSD treatment options, and Matthew elected WET because he thought that he might like the process of writing and preferred not to have between-session assignments, which other treatment options included. The therapist and Matthew scheduled the first WET session.

The first two sessions progressed well; Matthew followed the writing instructions and used the full 30 minutes of allotted writing time during each session. He reported to the therapist that, although it was emotionally difficult to recount the trauma experience, he found the writing sessions to be like "a weight being lifted." Just before the third session, Matthew contacted the therapist to cancel the upcoming session due to a bad fall on the ice in front of his home. The session was rescheduled for several days later. When Matthew presented for the third session, his right arm was in a cast and he reported that he fractured his right wrist in the fall. Because he was right-handed, he was unable to write for the remaining sessions. The therapist and Matthew agreed that he would complete the remaining sessions by talking into a digital recorder rather than writing. The sessions proceeded as usual with the exception that Matthew talked into a digital recorder. The therapist listened to the recorded sessions prior to each subsequent session and provided feedback, as usual.

His score on the PCL-5 after the last WET session was 12, indicating a substantial decrease in PTSD symptoms from baseline; in fact, it was unlikely that he met the diagnostic criteria for PTSD. Moreover, he reported feeling better than he had in years, noting that his sleep had significantly improved because he no longer experienced nightmares that awakened him on a regular basis. Matthew also indicated that he no longer felt guilty about not being able to save the woman who died; he now realized that there was nothing he could have done to prevent her death. The therapist and Matthew agreed that no additional sessions were needed and treatment was concluded.

We have treated clients who began treatment being unable to write because of a disability. In those cases, we followed the WET protocol, but the client used a digital recorder to recount the trauma narrative. The use of digital recorders in such cases has worked well. However, as described in Chapter 3, we recommend using a digital recorder only when the client is not physically able to write.

CASE 4: DISSOCIATION PRESENTATION

Some trauma survivors report dissociative symptoms, in addition to the core PTSD symptoms. In fact, prior research suggests that 15% to 30% of those with PTSD meet criteria for the dissociative subtype of PTSD (e.g., Stein et al., 2013). In the past, there has been some concerns about using exposure-based treatments with those who have dissociative tendencies because they may not be able to fully engage in in vivo exposure exercises without experiencing alterations in consciousness that might interfere with processing the trauma memory in a productive manner (Cloitre et al., 2012). However, research indicates that, in fact, PTSD clients with dissociative tendencies may experience the same benefits as those without such tendencies and that therapist concerns about dissociation interfering with therapy are overstated (De Jongh et al., 2016). There is no reason to think that PTSD clients with dissociative tendencies couldn't similarly benefit from WET. In fact, one of our clients, Barbara, experienced such dissociation when confronted by trauma reminders.

Barbara was a divorced, Hispanic woman in her 40s who presented for PTSD treatment related to a serious car accident she had experienced approximately 15 years earlier. Barbara was traveling with her two best friends when they had a head on collision that killed both of her friends and left Barbara seriously injured. Since the accident Barbara reported that she had significant interpersonal problems; she no longer wanted to have close relationships, isolated herself in her apartment due to fear of being injured, and was unable to work. Barbara was seen by a psychiatrist who prescribed several medications to manage her psychiatric symptoms. She had been taking these medications for a number of years with minimal benefit. Aside from seeing a psychiatrist, Barbara indicated she had never received psychotherapy because of a lack of financial resources and health insurance that did not cover psychotherapy sessions. An assessment of lifetime trauma experiences indicated several other events, including domestic violence involving her ex-husband. However, she clearly reported that the car accident was related to her PTSD symptoms. In addition to PTSD, based on administration of the mood disorders module of the Structured Diagnostic Interview for the *Diagnostic and Statistical Manual of Mental Disorders, Fourth Edition* (Spitzer, Williams, Gibbon, & First, 1994),

Barbara met diagnostic criteria for dysthymic disorder. Her score on the PCL-5 was 68. Several PTSD treatment options were discussed but she indicated a strong preference for WET; she wanted a treatment that would require fewer sessions because she experienced a great deal of distress when leaving her home. The therapist and Barbara agreed to conduct the first session of WET 1 week later.

Barbara presented on time for her first WET session. The therapist provided the rationale for treatment and then read the writing instructions. Barbara became very tearful when given the writing instructions because she was afraid to write about the car accident she typically went out of her way to avoid remembering. The therapist reiterated the rationale for the treatment and reminded Barbara that she was simply recounting the accident, not reliving it, and he noted the importance of this distinction. Barbara continued to want to discuss her fears about the writing, but the therapist correctly recognized her desire to discuss her fear as a means of avoiding the actual writing. The more Barbara talked about the process of writing, the more fearful and apprehensive she became. To reduce her anxiety and avoidance, the therapist asked Barbara quickly for a SUDS rating (which was 90) and told her to start the 30 minutes of writing. The therapist also indicated that he would keep track of the time and would return to the room when the 30 minutes were up.

After approximately 20 minutes, Barbara emerged from the room and told the therapist that she could not continue the writing. The therapist and Barbara went back into the room, where the therapist encouraged Barbara to continue writing for the remaining 10 minutes. Barbara reported that she simply could not tolerate writing about her experience. Understanding that Barbara could not be convinced to write any more, the therapist asked Barbara for her SUDS rating, which was 95. The therapist noticed that items on the desk that Barbara was sitting at were misplaced and knocked over. He asked her what had happened. Barbara stated that she wasn't sure what happened but that she may have been shaking the desk during the session. Barbara reported that the writing was a difficult experience for her because she felt as though the accident was happening again; it was not just a memory. She also indicated that she thought she might have "blacked out" during some of the session. After further inquiry, Barbara acknowledged that she sometimes "loses touch" with reality but that these experiences were somewhat infrequent and would last only a few minutes. The therapist suggested some techniques that Barbara could use to "ground" herself when she began to experience these dissociative occurrences. Barbara had not been aware that there were techniques she could use during these episodes and reported she would try using them at home as well as in future treatment sessions.

The therapist praised Barbara for completing the first writing session, especially in light of how much fear she reported at the beginning of the session. He also pointed out that Barbara was able to tolerate the high level of fear she experienced. Given her prior SUDS rating of 95, the therapist asked Barbara for another SUDS rating before ending the session, which Barbara reported as 75. Noting the decrease from the start of the writing, the therapist scheduled the second WET session and instructed Barbara that if she had thoughts, images, or feelings about the car accident during the upcoming week that she should allow herself to have them, whatever they might be.

The therapist read the first narrative, which consisted of three sentences. The first sentence started with a description of how Barbara and her two friends were driving home after dinner, and Barbara's two friends were in the front seat while Barbara sat in the back. The second sentence was incomplete with a description of bright lights, a loud noise, and burning smell. The third sentence consisted of just several words in all CAPS (e.g., "RED"). It appeared to the therapist that Barbara became quickly overwhelmed with the writing and that the dissociative experience occurred early in the course of the writing session. When Barbara presented for the second writing session, the therapist talked with her more about what had occurred during the first writing session given that she was only able to write a few sentences. Barbara acknowledged that she felt overwhelmed at the start of the writing and was not able to move forward past the first couple of sentences. Given this, the therapist offered to remain in the room with her to assist in "grounding" her in the event she dissociated again. Barbara agreed that having the therapist remain in the room would likely be helpful. He emphasized that he would simply sit in the room and would not interact with Barbara, unless it was necessary for her to continue writing.

The therapist read the second writing session instructions to Barbara and asked her for a SUDS rating, which was 90. The therapist then prompted Barbara to begin writing for 30 minutes and told her that he would let her know when she should stop writing. Barbara then proceeded with writing while the therapist remained in the room. About 15 minutes into the session, Barbara became visibly upset, and the therapist thought she might be dissociating. He instructed her to keep her feet flat on the floor and to grab the left corner of the desk with her left hand. Barbara followed these instructions and appeared to become less distressed. Although she stopped writing for several minutes, she began to write again after being given the grounding instructions. After 30 minutes, the therapist told Barbara to stop writing. She reported her SUDS following writing as 75. The therapist then asked Barbara how this writing session went for her. She reported that although she still found the process of writing very upsetting, it was easier than the previous session. The therapist remarked that her SUDS rating suggested that she was less distressed than the first writing session. Barbara noted that she was amazed that she was able to write as much about the accident and that this was the first time since the accident that she allowed herself to think about it to this extent. The therapist again praised Barbara for completing the session and remarked that she was stronger than she thought. Barbara agreed that she likely underestimated her strength and ability to accomplish challenges. The therapist reminded Barbara to allow herself to have whatever images, thoughts, or feelings about the accident that came up rather than trying to push them away. Barbara acknowledged that it would be a challenge for her to follow this instruction but that she would try. The session ended.

Barbara presented for the third session, reporting that it was helpful for her to have the therapist remain in the room while she wrote during the previous session and that she would like the therapist to remain in the room for the session. The therapist agreed to remain in the room and let Barbara know he had read her trauma narrative and was impressed by how much she was able to write about the event, especially compared with what she was able to accomplish in the first session. He also remarked how well she did with including details of the accident. He did note that she didn't write much about her thoughts and feelings about the accident and that it would be important for her to do so in this session. Barbara agreed with this assessment of her trauma narrative and said she would do her best to write about her thoughts and feelings.

The therapist then read the instructions for the third writing session, took a SUDS rating from Barbara, which was 75, and prompted her to start writing. This session was similar to the second writing session in that Barbara became quite upset in the middle of the trauma writing at which time she stopped writing and seemed to be dissociating. However, before the therapist could provide grounding instructions, Barbara began using a grounding technique that the therapist had told her about previously, which was to snap a rubber band that was around her wrist. The therapist noted that after snapping the rubber band several times, Barbara became more focused and continued with her writing. At the end of the 30 minutes of writing, the therapist instructed Barbara to stop writing and took her SUDS rating, which was 65. The therapist asked Barbara about using the rubber band grounding technique and she reported that she had started to use this technique between sessions and found it helpful in grounding her when she began to dissociate at home. The therapist praised Barbara for being proactive in using grounding techniques between sessions. They then discussed the process of writing that session, which Barbara reported as still difficult but easier than prior sessions. She also noted that she had written about some of her thoughts and feelings in the current session. The therapist then gave Barbara the instructions not to avoid thoughts, images, and feelings about the accident if they should occur during the course of the week, and the session was ended.

A review of Barbara's third narrative was consistent with her reporting that she had written, to some extent, about her thoughts and feelings. When Barbara presented for the next session she reported that she had eaten dinner out with a friend twice in the prior week, which was very unusual for her. She credited going out to dinner as the result of having had a positive experience confronting her trauma memory and realizing that she needed to start to confront other things in her life that she had been avoiding as a result of the car accident. The therapist praised Barbara for taking these positive steps. Because she had done well in the prior session, they agreed that the therapist would not remain in the room for that session. The therapist read the instructions for the fourth writing session and asked Barbara for a SUDS rating, which was 60. She was prompted to begin writing with the reminder that the therapist would track her time and return after 30 minutes. After 30 minutes, the therapist returned to the room and prompted Barbara to stop writing. She provided a SUDS rating of 55, which was consistent with a gradual reduction in SUDS over the course of the sessions; the therapist noted this to Barbara. Barbara reported that the sessions seemed to get progressively easier and that she had less frequent dissociative experiences over the course of the sessions. She attributed the decrease in dissociation to a combination of learning ground techniques and feeling less fearful about confronting her trauma memory.

The last writing session proceeded in a similar fashion as Session 4. Barbara's PCL-5 score at the last session was 43, which was a notable reduction from her pretreatment score of 68. However, her score was still relatively high and indicative of severe PTSD symptoms. The score was consistent with Barbara's own observations that although she had received some benefits from treatment, she could still use some additional treatment. The therapist suggested that they continue PTSD treatment together either by conducting additional WET sessions or trying a different trauma-focused approach, such as prolonged exposure. In particular, given the high number of avoidance behaviors that Barbara engaged in and that caused her significant impairment, the therapist thought the in vivo exposure component of prolonged exposure might be particularly helpful. Barbara reported that she was satisfied with the treatment benefit she had received from WET and noted that she had started to confront situations, people, and places she had been avoiding following the car accident. She believed she could continue to make progress on her own without additional treatment sessions. The therapist respected Barbara's preference but let her know that she could return for treatment should she change her mind or experience a relapse.

CASE 5: RESISTANCE TO TRAUMA-FOCUSED TREATMENT

As we saw from the last case example, many of those who suffer from PTSD are reluctant to confront their traumatic memories. Although some of them overcome their fears and fully engage in treatment, like Barbara, there are others who remain either unwilling or unable to engage even with lots of therapist encouragement. This final case example describes such a client.

John was a divorced, male veteran in his 50s who presented for PTSD treatment related to military sexual trauma that occurred 30 years prior. John indicated that he had been sexually assaulted by two fellow soldiers during his military service. He stated that he did not report the assault because he felt shame and sensed that reporting the event would have had a negative outcome for him. He reported that he had presented for PTSD treatment several times in the past and had received prolonged exposure, cognitive processing therapy, and supportive counseling. However, he had not perceived treatment to be helpful and terminated each of these courses of treatment prematurely. In addition to meeting diagnostic criteria for PTSD, John also had a lengthy substance use disorder history. However, he reported only moderate alcohol consumption at the time of this treatment presentation.

Several treatment options were discussed with John; he elected to try WET because he wanted to do something other than what he had done before, found the idea of writing about the trauma appealing, and liked the idea that there would be no between-session assignments. John's PCL-5 at the initial session was 49, indicating probable PTSD of relatively high severity.

At the first WET session, the therapist checked with John to make sure he hadn't changed his mind regarding his treatment preference. John confirmed that he wanted to proceed with WET. The therapist then explained the treatment rationale and provide PTSD psychoeducation material to John. The therapist also read the writing instructions for the first session. John indicated that he understood the instructions and was ready to start writing. The therapist then took a SUDS rating from John, which was 35. She let John know that she would keep track of time and that in 30 minutes she would return to the room to prompt him to stop writing.

After 30 minutes the therapist returned to the room to let John know that he should stop writing. She took a SUDS rating from John according to how he was feeling in that moment and John provided a rating of 40. The therapist then inquired how the writing session went for John. He stated that he had not been able to write very much; he found it difficult to write about the assault he experienced because it was distressing for him to recount the event. The therapist asked John what he had been doing during the session if he was not spending the time writing. John reported that he spent time thinking about what he could or would write but decided that it just was not something he felt able to do. The therapist asked John if he wanted to proceed with the treatment; John indicated that he did want to continue as he felt he would be able to do the writing in the next session. The therapist then scheduled the second WET session with John and gave him the instruction that he should not try to suppress any thoughts, images, or feelings he might have about the event, whatever they might be. John stated that he would do his best.

After the session the therapist reviewed the narrative. John had written a couple of pages that mainly focused on the events of the day leading up to the assault. However, once John got to the assault he seemed to have stopped writing. When John returned for the second WET session the therapist noted that he seemed to have spent more time writing than he had indicated to the therapist but noted that he also seemed to stop writing once he got to the part in his narrative in which he was assaulted. John agreed with this assessment and indicated that he felt ready to write about the trauma event at this session. The therapist then read the instructions for Session 2, took John's SUDS rating (which was 30), and prompted him to begin writing.

After 30 minutes the therapist returned to the room and prompted John to stop writing. A SUDS rating was taken, which John reported as 30, and the therapist asked how the session went. John acknowledged that he had difficulty writing about the assault. He questioned the point of writing about the narrative, to which the therapist provided the rationale for confronting the trauma memory. She asked John about the difficulty that he was having, to which he replied that he just did not like to think about the assault and could not bring himself to do so, even though he understood why it would be helpful to do so. The therapist noted that the low SUDS ratings both before and after the writing in the first two sessions indicated that John was continuing to avoid the trauma memory and that he would need to recount the traumatic memory to benefit from the treatment. Furthermore, his PCL-5 score at the second session was similar to his pretreatment score. She again checked with John about whether it made sense to proceed with the treatment if he was unwilling to write about the trauma. John stated that he did not want to give up trying and that he would return the following week ready to "get to work." After she instructed John not to avoid distressing thoughts and images he might experience regarding the trauma event between sessions, they scheduled the next session.

Following the session, the therapist reviewed John's narrative. Although he did begin to write about the sexual assault, he only wrote a few sentences. Moreover, unlike his logical, clear, and detailed narrative written in the first session, the narrative from the second session consisted of incomplete sentences ("sweaty blond hair," "smelled like cigarettes"). When John returned for the third WET session he stated that he was willing to continue with the treatment but wanted the therapist to know that he would not be able to write about the assault. The therapist pointed out that if he was not willing to write about the assault, they could not proceed with the treatment. John stated that he respected the therapist's decision not to continue on with WET. The therapist then discussed with John his goals for treatment, which was PTSD symptom reduction (e.g., fewer nightmares, less avoidance behaviors, less anger, better relationships). The therapist explained that to achieve these treatment goals he would need to confront his trauma memory. John stated that he was willing to "deal with" his symptoms rather than allow himself to think about what had happened to him. Given John's resistance to trauma-focused treatment, which included his treatment history of prematurely dropping out of other trauma-focused treatments, the therapist offered John alternative treatment options. John and the therapist agreed that anger management group treatment would be a good alternative treatment option because it would provide John with skills to better manage his chronic anger and would provide social interaction with individuals who have experienced traumatic events. The social interaction would be beneficial in terms of reducing his social isolation. John was then referred to the anger management group and individual treatment was terminated.

It is not atypical for some clients to simply not be willing to confront their trauma memories, no matter how skilled the therapist is at explaining why doing so would be beneficial. Effective trauma-focused therapy relies on engagement of both the client and the therapist. If a client who shows up for sessions is unwilling to engage in treatment, then it is not wise to try to continue to work on rapport building in the hopes that the client will come around and begin to engage in the treatment. It is much better to terminate trauma-focused treatment with an unwilling client and pursue a different treatment path than to forge ahead with trying to conduct trauma-focused treatment sessions when the client is unwilling. Clients who are not ready to engage in trauma-focused treatment but who have a generally positive sense of these treatments might return at a later date when they feel they are ready to move forward. However, if they complete a course of trauma-focused treatment in which they never completed between-session assignments or engaged in the work within the sessions, then they will leave the treatment with the impression that treatment does not work. In such cases, they are less likely to try the treatment again in the future when they may be more able to engage with the treatment.

Although John was not willing to confront his trauma memory, the majority of clients are willing to do so. It's not atypical for clients to display some reluctance to engage in imaginal exposure. However, a supportive and encouraging clinician can manage such reluctance. For those clients who are willing to move forward with WET, they are pleasantly surprised to find that writing about their traumatic memory is not as aversive as they feared it might be. Moreover, they experience treatment gains in a short amount of time without conducting assignments between the sessions. The client completes the five sessions of WET feeling that a weight has been lifted and that he or she is in a position to reengage with relationships, perform well at work, and have an enhanced sense of enjoyment from life.

Appendix

WRITTEN EXPOSURE THERAPY SCRIPT

SESSION 1

Introduction to Written Exposure Treatment

Survivors of traumatic experiences often go through changes in their physical reactions, emotions, thoughts, and behaviors in the wake of such experiences.

Examples of changes in physical reactions may include increased fatigue, nausea (feeling sick to your stomach), sweating or chills, shock, dizziness, chest pains, trouble breathing, and numbness.

Examples of emotional changes may include increased nervousness, fear, grief, depression, hopelessness, helplessness, anger, irritability, feeling overwhelmed, guilt, and vulnerability.

Examples of changes in thinking may include increased thinking that your future will be cut short, difficulty in remembering things, trouble making decisions, confusion, difficulty concentrating, "flashbacks" or reliving experiences, nightmares, intrusive or unwelcome thoughts, too many thoughts at once, thinking about suicide, and memory gaps.

Examples of changes in behavior may include increased startle, hypervigilance, being withdrawn from others, being overly dependent upon others, changes in appetite, changes in sleep, increased substance abuse (alcohol, drugs, medication), problems with emotional or physical intimacy, inability to trust or have loving feelings, apathy, loss of spirituality, risk taking, and suicidal impulses and behaviors.

Each person may differ in the ways in which these reactions are experienced. Some may be very familiar but others may not. Many of these reactions become part of the trauma survivor's everyday life and do not seem unusual to him or her. Take a moment to think about how many of the above symptoms you experienced since the traumatic event.

The manner in which a survivor attempts to cope with his or her trauma symptoms also has an impact on everyday activities. If a trauma survivor has recurring thoughts and memories of a trauma, he or she may attempt to avoid them by using substances (alcohol and/or drugs), becoming a workaholic, staying away from other people, or using anger and aggressive behavior to either distract oneself or remove any reminders of the trauma from the current circumstances. These strategies may give the trauma survivor short-term relief but over the long-term can be problematic for a variety of reasons. In other words, sometimes a survivor's attempt to cure or to cope with reactions to a traumatic event can become a problem in and of itself.

Importantly, approaches that one might use to deal with nontraumatic events do not work very well in dealing with trauma. People will sometimes tell trauma survivors to "forget about it" and to get on with their lives. This approach may work well in many different situations, but one does not just forget about traumatic events.

One of the reasons that this advice does not work is that events that are experienced as traumatic are remembered differently from nontraumatic events. The memory of a trauma may be stored in a splintered fashion as a protection from reexperiencing the full impact of the trauma. Consequently, survivors may have amnesia for large segments of time surrounding the trauma. Or they may remember some details of past traumas but may not have any feelings attached to these memories. They may experience overwhelming anxiety or fearfulness without understanding the cause. Certain situations may trigger "flashbacks" to earlier traumas, and they might feel that they are actually reliving the past.

To successfully recover from the traumatic event, it is important that you confront that experience by recounting it, repeatedly, in as much detail and with as much emotion as possible. By repeatedly recounting the event, you will be able to correct for the splintered fashion in which the memory may have been stored. You will also find that recounting the experience will result in you feeling like you have more control over the memory rather than feeling as if the memory controls you. Over the next several sessions, I will be asking you to repeatedly recount the trauma experience by writing about the experience.

General Directions for Writing Sessions and Specific Instructions for Session 1

Over the next five sessions I would like you to write about your trauma. Don't worry about your spelling or grammar. I would like you to write about the details of the trauma as you remember it now—for example, how the trauma event happened and whether other people were involved. In writing about the details of the trauma, it is important to write about specifics of what happened and what you were feeling and thinking as the trauma was happening. Try to be as specific in recounting the details as possible. It is also important that you really let go and explore your very deepest emotions and thoughts about the trauma. You should also keep in mind that you have five sessions to write about this experience, so you don't need to be concerned with completing your account of the trauma within today's session. Just be sure to be as detailed about the trauma as possible and also to write about your thoughts and feelings as you remember them during (and immediately after) the trauma.

For your first writing session, I'd like you to write about the trauma starting at the beginning. For instance, you could begin with the moment you realized the trauma was about to happen. As you describe the trauma, it is important that you provide as many specific details as you can remember. For example, you might write about what you saw (e.g., headlights of the car approaching you, person approaching you), what you heard (e.g., car horn, screeching tires, person threatening you, explosion), or what you smelled (e.g., blood, burning rubber). In addition to writing about the details of the trauma, you should also be writing about your thoughts and feelings during the trauma as you remember it now. For example, you might have had the thought, "I'm going to die," "This can't be happening," or "I'm going to be raped." And you might have felt terrified, frozen with fear, or angry at another person involved.

Remember, you don't need to finish writing about the entire trauma in this session. Just focus on writing about the trauma with as much detail as possible and include the thoughts and feelings you experienced during and immediately after the trauma. Remember, the trauma is not actually happening again, you are simply recounting it as you look back upon it now.

Instructions for Concluding Session 1

You will likely have thoughts, images, and feelings concerning the trauma you just wrote about during the course of the upcoming week. It is important that you allow yourself to have these thoughts, images, and feelings, whatever they might be, rather than trying to push them away. Please try to allow yourself to have whatever thoughts, images, and feelings that may come up.

SESSION 2

Writing Instructions for Session 2

Today, I want you to continue to write about the trauma as you look back upon it now. If you feel that you didn't get the chance to completely describe the trauma in the last writing session, then you can pick up where you left off. If you completed writing about the trauma event in the last session, please write about the entire trauma again. While you are describing the trauma, I really want you to delve into your very deepest feelings (e.g., fear, shock, sadness, anger) and thoughts (e.g., "Is this really happening?" "I'm going to die"). Also, remember to write about the details of the trauma. That is, describe the setting; the people involved; and what you saw, heard, and felt. Remember that you are writing about the trauma as you look back upon it now.

Instructions for Concluding Session 2

As I stated at the end of the first session, you will likely have thoughts, feelings, and visual images concerning the trauma during the course of the upcoming week. It is important that you allow yourself to have these thoughts, images, and feelings, whatever they might be, rather than trying to push them away. Please try to allow yourself to have whatever thoughts, images, and feelings that come up.

SESSION 3

Writing Instructions for Session 3

In your writing today, I again want you to continue writing about the trauma event as you think about it today. If you have completed writing about the entire trauma you experienced, you can either write about the trauma again from the beginning or you can select a part of the trauma that is most upsetting to you and focus your writing on that specific part of the experience. In addition, I would also like you to begin to write about how the traumatic experience has changed your life. For instance, you might write about whether or not the trauma has changed the way you view your life, the meaning of life, and how you relate to other people. Throughout your writing, I want you to really let go and write about your deepest thoughts and feelings.

Instructions for Concluding Session 3

As I've stated previously, you will likely have thoughts, feelings, and visual images concerning the trauma during the course of the upcoming week. It is important that you allow yourself to have these thoughts, images, and feelings, whatever they might be, rather than trying to push them away. Please try to allow yourself to have whatever thoughts, images, and feelings that come up.

SESSION 4

Writing Instructions for Session 4

I want you to continue to write about the trauma today. As with your writing in the last session, you can select a specific part of the trauma to write about; that is, the part of the trauma that was most upsetting to you. Today, I would also like you to write about how the trauma event has changed your life. You might write about if the trauma has changed the way you view your life, the meaning of life, and how you relate to other people. Throughout the session I want you to really let go and write about your deepest thoughts and feelings.

Instructions for Concluding Session 4

As I've stated previously, you will likely have thoughts, feelings, and visual images concerning the trauma during the course of this week. It is important that you allow yourself to have these thoughts, images, and feelings, whatever they might be, rather than trying to push them away. Please try to allow yourself to have whatever thoughts, images, and feelings that come up.

SESSION 5

Today is the last session. I want you to continue to write about your feelings and thoughts related to the traumatic event and how you believe this event has changed your life. Remember that this is the last day of writing, so you might want to try to wrap up your writing. For example, you might write about how the traumatic experience is related to your current life and your future. As with the other writing sessions, it is important for you to delve into your deepest emotions and thoughts throughout the session.

References

Addis, M. E., & Carpenter, K. M. (2000). The treatment rationale in cognitive behavioral therapy: Psychological mechanisms and clinical guidelines. *Cognitive and Behavioral Practice, 7*, 147–156. http://dx.doi.org/10.1016/S1077-7229(00)80025-5

Aderka, I. M., Gillihan, S. J., McLean, C. P., & Foa, E. B. (2013). The relationship between posttraumatic and depressive symptoms during prolonged exposure with and without cognitive restructuring for the treatment of posttraumatic stress disorder. *Journal of Consulting and Clinical Psychology, 81*, 375–382. http://dx.doi.org/10.1037/a0031523

Alcántara, C., Casement, M. D., & Lewis-Fernández, R. (2013). Conditional risk for PTSD among Latinos: A systematic review of racial/ethnic differences and sociocultural explanations. *Clinical Psychology Review, 33*, 107–119. http://dx.doi.org/10.1016/j.cpr.2012.10.005

American Psychiatric Association. (1994). *Diagnostic and statistical manual of mental disorders* (4th ed.). Washington, DC: Author.

American Psychiatric Association. (2013). *Diagnostic and statistical manual of mental disorders* (5th ed.). Arlington, VA: Author.

American Psychological Association. (2017). *Ethical principles of psychologists and code of conduct* (2002, Amended June 1, 2010 and January 1, 2017). Retrieved from http://www.apa.org/ethics/code/index.aspx

Bachynski, K. E., Canham-Chervak, M., Black, S. A., Dada, E. O., Millikan, A. M., & Jones, B. H. (2012). Mental health risk factors for suicides in the US Army, 2007–8. *Injury Prevention, 18*, 405–412. http://dx.doi.org/10.1136/injuryprev-2011-040112

Baker, A. S., Litwack, S. D., Clapp, J. D., Beck, J. G., & Sloan, D. M. (2014). The Driving Behavior Survey as a measure of behavioral stress responses to MVA-related PTSD. *Behavior Therapy, 45*, 443–453. http://dx.doi.org/10.1016/j.beth.2014.02.009

Beck, A. T., Steer, R. A., & Brown, G. K. (1996). *Manual for the Beck Depression Inventory–II*. San Antonio, TX: Psychological Corporation.

Becker, C. B., Zayfert, C., & Anderson, E. (2004). A survey of psychologists' attitudes towards and utilization of exposure therapy for PTSD. *Behaviour Research and Therapy, 42,* 277–292. http://dx.doi.org/10.1016/S0005-7967(03)00138-4

Ben-Porath, Y. S., & Tellegen, A. (2011). *Minnesota Multiphasic Personality Inventory–2–Restructured Form® (MMPI-2-RF®): User's guide for reports* (2nd ed.). Minneapolis: University of Minnesota Press.

Blake, D. D., Weathers, F. W., Nagy, L. M., Kaloupek, D. G., Charney, D. S., & Keane, T. M. (1990). *The Clinician Administered PTSD Scale–IV.* Boston, MA: National Center for PTSD, Behavioral Sciences Division.

Blanchard, E. B., & Hickling, E. J. (2004). *After the crash: Assessment and treatment of motor vehicle accident survivors* (2nd ed.). Washington, DC: American Psychological Association. http://dx.doi.org/10.1037/10676-000

Blanchard, E. B., Hickling, E. J., Devineni, T., Veazey, C. H., Galovski, T. E., Mundy, E., . . . Buckley, T. C. (2003). A controlled evaluation of cognitive behavioural therapy for posttraumatic stress in motor vehicle accident survivors. *Behaviour Research and Therapy, 41,* 79–96. http://dx.doi.org/10.1016/S0005-7967(01)00131-0

Borah, E. V., Wright, E. C., Donahue, D. A., Cedillos, E. M., Riggs, D. S., Isler, W. C., & Peterson, A. L. (2013). Implementation outcomes of military provider training in cognitive processing therapy and prolonged exposure therapy for post-traumatic stress disorder. *Military Medicine, 178,* 939–944. http://dx.doi.org/10.7205/MILMED-D-13-00072

Bouton, M. E. (2004). Context and behavioral processes in extinction. *Learning & Memory, 11,* 485–494. http://dx.doi.org/10.1101/lm.78804

Bovin, M. J., Marx, B. P., Weathers, F. W., Gallagher, M. W., Rodriguez, P., Schnurr, P. P., & Keane, T. M. (2016). Psychometric properties of the PTSD Checklist for *Diagnostic and Statistical Manual of Mental Disorders–Fifth Edition* (PCL-5) in veterans. *Psychological Assessment, 28,* 1379–1391. http://dx.doi.org/10.1037/pas0000254

Bradley, R., Greene, J., Russ, E., Dutra, L., & Westen, D. (2005). A multi-dimensional meta-analysis of psychotherapy for PTSD. *The American Journal of Psychiatry, 162,* 214–227. http://dx.doi.org/10.1176/appi.ajp.162.2.214

Breslau, N., Davis, G. C., Andreski, P., & Peterson, E. (1991). Traumatic events and posttraumatic stress disorder in an urban population of young adults. *Archives of General Psychiatry, 48,* 216–222. http://dx.doi.org/10.1001/archpsyc.1991.01810270028003

Bryan, C. J., May, A. M., Rozek, D. C., Williams, S. R., Clemans, T. A., Mintz, J., . . . Burch, T. S. (2018). Use of crisis management interventions among suicidal patients: Results of a randomized controlled trial. *Depression and Anxiety, 35,* 619–628. http://dx.doi.org/10.1002/da.22753

Bryant, R. A., Ekasawin, S., Chakrabhand, S., Suwanmitri, S., Duangchun, O., & Chantaluckwong, T. (2011). A randomized controlled effectiveness trial of cognitive behavior therapy for post-traumatic stress disorder in terrorist-affected people in Thailand. *World Psychiatry, 10,* 205–209. http://dx.doi.org/ 10.1002/j.2051-5545.2011.tb00058.x

Bryant, R. A., Moulds, M. L., Guthrie, R. M., Dang, S. T., Mastrodomenico, J., Nixon, R. D., . . . Creamer, M. (2008). A randomized controlled trial of exposure therapy and cognitive restructuring for posttraumatic stress disorder. *Journal of Consulting and Clinical Psychology, 76,* 695–703. http:// dx.doi.org/10.1037/a0012616

Bryant, R. A., Moulds, M. L., Guthrie, R. M., Dang, S. T., & Nixon, R. D. (2003). Imaginal exposure alone and imaginal exposure with cognitive restructuring in treatment of posttraumatic stress disorder. *Journal of Consulting and Clinical Psychology, 71,* 706–712. http://dx.doi.org/10.1037/0022-006X.71.4.706

Cahill, S. P., Rothbaum, B. O., Resick, P. A., & Follette, V. M. (2009). Cognitive behavioral therapy for adults. In E. B. Foa, T. M. Keane, M. J. Friedman, and J. A. Cohen (Eds.), *Effective treatments for PTSD: Practice guidelines form the international society for traumatic stress studies* (pp. 139–222). New York, NY: Guilford Press.

Charney, M. E., & Keane, T. M. (2007). Psychometric analyses of the Clinician-Administered PTSD Scale (CAPS)—Bosnian translation. *Cultural Diversity and Ethnic Minority Psychology, 13,* 161–168. http://dx.doi.org/10.1037/ 1099-9809.13.2.161

Clapp, J. D., Olsen, S. A., Beck, J. G., Palyo, S. A., Grant, D. M., Gudmundsdottir, B., & Marques, L. (2011). The Driving Behavior Survey: Scale construction and validation. *Journal of Anxiety Disorders, 25,* 96–105. http://dx.doi.org/ 10.1016/j.janxdis.2010.08.008

Cloitre, M., Courtois, C. A., Ford, J. D., Green, B. L., Alexander, P., Briere, J., . . . Van der Hart, O. (2012). *The ISTSS expert consensus treatment guidelines for complex PTSD in adults.* Chicago, IL: International Society for Traumatic Stress Studies.

Craske, M. G., Treanor, M., Conway, C. C., Zbozinek, T., & Vervliet, B. (2014). Maximizing exposure therapy: An inhibitory learning approach. *Behaviour Research and Therapy, 58,* 10–23. http://dx.doi.org/10.1016/ j.brat.2014.04.006

Cusack, K., Jonas, D. E., Forneris, C. A., Wines, C., Sonis, J., Middleton, J. C., . . . Weil, A. (2016). *Psychological treatments for adults with posttraumatic stress disorder: A systematic review and meta-analysis.* Santa Monica, CA: RAND Corporation.

de Jong, J. T., Komproe, I. H., Van Ommeren, M., El Masri, M., Araya, M., Khaled, N., . . . Somasundaram, D. (2001). Lifetime events and posttraumatic stress disorder in 4 postconflict settings. *JAMA, 286,* 555–562. http:// dx.doi.org/10.1001/jama.286.5.555

De Jongh, A., Resick, P. A., Zoellner, L. A., van Minnen, A., Lee, C. W., Monson, C. M., . . . Bicanic, I. A. E. (2016). A critical analysis of the current treatment guidelines for complex PTSD in adults. *Depression and Anxiety, 33,* 359–369. http://dx.doi.org/10.1002/da.22469

Eftekhari, A., Ruzek, J. I., Crowley, J. J., Rosen, C. S., Greenbaum, M. A., & Karlin, B. E. (2013). Effectiveness of national implementation of prolonged exposure therapy in Veterans Affairs care. *JAMA Psychiatry, 70*, 949–955. http://dx.doi.org/10.1001/jamapsychiatry.2013.36

Ehlers, A., Clark, D. M., Hackmann, A., McManus, F., & Fennell, M. (2005). Cognitive therapy for post-traumatic stress disorder: Development and evaluation. *Behaviour Research and Therapy, 43*, 413–431. http://dx.doi.org/10.1016/j.brat.2004.03.006

Ehlers, A., Hackmann, A., Grey, N., Wild, J., Liness, S., Albert, I., . . . Clark, D. M. (2014). A randomized controlled trial of 7-day intensive and standard weekly cognitive therapy for PTSD and emotion-focused supportive therapy. *The American Journal of Psychiatry, 171*, 294–304. http://dx.doi.org/10.1176/appi.ajp.2013.13040552

Ehlers, A., Mayou, R. A., & Bryant, B. (2003). Cognitive predictors of post-traumatic stress disorder in children: Results of a prospective longitudinal study. *Behaviour Research and Therapy, 41*, 1–10. http://dx.doi.org/10.1016/S0005-7967(01)00126-7

Epstein, E. M., Sloan, D. M., & Marx, B. P. (2005). Getting to the heart of the matter: Written disclosure, gender, and heart rate. *Psychosomatic Medicine, 67*, 413–419. http://dx.doi.org/10.1097/01.psy.0000160474.82170.7b

Ertl, V., Pfeiffer, A., Schauer, E., Elbert, T., & Neuner, F. (2011). Community-implemented trauma therapy for former child soldiers in Northern Uganda: A randomized controlled trial. *Journal of the American Medical Association, 306*, 503–512. http://dx.doi.org/10.1001/jama.2011.1060

Finley, E. P., Garcia, H. A., Ketchum, N. S., McGeary, D. D., McGeary, C. A., Stirman, S. W., & Peterson, A. L. (2015). Utilization of evidence-based psychotherapies in Veterans Affairs posttraumatic stress disorder outpatient clinics. *Psychological Services, 12*, 73–82. http://dx.doi.org/10.1037/ser0000014

First, M. B., Williams, J. B. W., Karg, R. S., & Spitzer, R. L. (2016). *Structured Clinical Interview for* DSM–5 *Disorders, clinical version (SCID–5–CV)*. Arlington, VA: American Psychiatric Association.

Foa, E. B., Hembree, E. A., Cahill, S. P., Rauch, S. A., Riggs, D. S., Feeny, N. C., & Yadin, E. (2005). Randomized trial of prolonged exposure for posttraumatic stress disorder with and without cognitive restructuring: Outcome at academic and community clinics. *Journal of Consulting and Clinical Psychology, 73*, 953–964. http://dx.doi.org/10.1037/0022-006X.73.5.953

Foa, E. B., Hembree, E., & Rothbaum, B. O. (2007). *Prolonged exposure therapy for PTSD: Emotional processing of traumatic experiences therapist guide.* New York, NY: Oxford University Press. http://dx.doi.org/10.1093/med:psych/9780195308501.001.0001

Foa, E. B., Keane, T. M., Friedman, M. J., & Cohen, J. (2008). *Effective treatments for PTSD: Practice guidelines from the International Society for Traumatic Stress Studies.* New York, NY: Guilford Press.

Frattaroli, J. (2006). Experimental disclosure and its moderators: A meta-analysis. *Psychological Bulletin, 132,* 823–865. http://dx.doi.org/10.1037/0033-2909.132.6.823

Fulton, J. J., Calhoun, P. S., Wagner, H. R., Schry, A. R., Hair, L. P., Feeling, N., . . . Beckham, J. C. (2015). The prevalence of posttraumatic stress disorder in Operation Enduring Freedom/Operation Iraqi Freedom (OEF/OIF) Veterans: A meta-analysis. *Journal of Anxiety Disorders, 31,* 98–107. http://dx.doi.org/10.1016/j.janxdis.2015.02.003

Galovski, T. E., Blain, L. M., Mott, J. M., Elwood, L., & Houle, T. (2012). Manualized therapy for PTSD: Flexing the structure of cognitive processing therapy. *Journal of Consulting and Clinical Psychology, 80,* 968–981. http://dx.doi.org/10.1037/a0030600

Garcia, H. A., Kelley, L. P., Rentz, T. O., & Lee, S. (2011). Pretreatment predictors of dropout from cognitive behavioral therapy for PTSD in Iraq and Afghanistan war veterans. *Psychological Services, 8,* 1–11. http://dx.doi.org/10.1037/a0022705

Gersons, B. P., Carlier, I. V., Lamberts, R. D., & van der Kolk, B. A. (2000). Randomized clinical trial of brief eclectic psychotherapy for police officers with posttraumatic stress disorder. *Journal of Traumatic Stress, 13,* 333–347. http://dx.doi.org/10.1023/A:1007793803627

Goldstein, R. B., Smith, S. M., Chou, S. P., Saha, T. D., Jung, J., Zhang, H., . . . Grant, B. F. (2016). The epidemiology of *DSM–5* posttraumatic stress disorder in the United States: Results from the National Epidemiologic Survey on Alcohol and Related Conditions–III. *Social Psychiatry and Psychiatric Epidemiology, 51,* 1137–1148. http://dx.doi.org/10.1007/s00127-016-1208-5

Gradus, J. L., Suvak, M. K., Wisco, B. E., Marx, B. P., & Resick, P. A. (2013). Treatment of posttraumatic stress disorder reduces suicidal ideation. *Depression and Anxiety, 30,* 1046–1053.

Gutner, C. A., Gallagher, M. W., Baker, A. S., Sloan, D. M., & Resick, P. A. (2016). Time course of treatment dropout in cognitive-behavioral therapies for posttraumatic stress disorder. *Psychological Trauma: Theory, Research, Practice, and Policy, 8,* 115–121. http://dx.doi.org/10.1037/tra0000062

Gutner, C. A., Suvak, M. K., Sloan, D. M., & Resick, P. A. (2016). Does timing matter? Examining the impact of session timing on outcome. *Journal of Consulting and Clinical Psychology, 84,* 1108–1115. http://dx.doi.org/10.1037/ccp0000120

Hamblen, J. L., Schnurr, P. P., Rosenberg, A., & Eftekhari, A. (2009). A guide to the literature on psychotherapy for PTSD. *Psychiatric Annals, 39,* 348–354. http://dx.doi.org/10.3928/00485713-20090515-02

Harned, M. S., Rizvi, S. L., & Linehan, M. M. (2010). Impact of co-occurring posttraumatic stress disorder on suicidal women with borderline personality disorder. *The American Journal of Psychiatry, 167,* 1210–1217. http://dx.doi.org/10.1176/appi.ajp.2010.09081213

Hatcher, R. L., & Gillaspy, J. A. (2006). Development and validation of a revised short version of the Working Alliance Inventory. *Psychotherapy Research, 16,* 12–25. http://dx.doi.org/10.1080/10503300500352500

Hembree, E. A., Foa, E. B., Dorfan, N. M., Street, G. P., Kowalski, J., & Tu, X. (2003). Do patients drop out prematurely from exposure therapy for PTSD? *Journal of Traumatic Stress, 16,* 555–562. http://dx.doi.org/10.1023/B:JOTS.0000004078.93012.7d

Herschell, A. D., Kolko, D. J., Baumann, B. L., & Davis, A. C. (2010). The role of therapist training in the implementation of psychosocial treatments: A review and critique with recommendations. *Clinical Psychology Review, 30,* 448–466. http://dx.doi.org/10.1016/j.cpr.2010.02.005

Hoge, C. W., & Chard, K. M. (2018). A window into the evolution of trauma-focused psychotherapies for posttraumatic stress disorder. *JAMA, 319,* 343–345. http://dx.doi.org/10.1001/jama.2017.21880

Imel, Z. E., Laska, K., Jakupcak, M., & Simpson, T. L. (2013). Meta-analysis of dropout in treatments for posttraumatic stress disorder. *Journal of Consulting and Clinical Psychology, 81,* 394–404. http://dx.doi.org/10.1037/a0031474

Karlin, B. E., Ruzek, J. I., Chard, K. M., Eftekhari, A., Monson, C. M., Hembree, E. A., . . . Foa, E. B. (2010). Dissemination of evidence-based psychological treatments for posttraumatic stress disorder in the Veterans Health Administration. *Journal of Traumatic Stress, 23,* 663–673. http://dx.doi.org/10.1002/jts.20588

Kazdin, A. E. (2017). Addressing the treatment gap: A key challenge for extending evidence-based psychosocial interventions. *Behaviour Research and Therapy, 88,* 7–18. http://dx.doi.org/10.1016/j.brat.2016.06.004

Kehle-Forbes, S. M., Meis, L. A., Spoont, M. R., & Polusny, M. A. (2016). Treatment initiation and dropout from prolonged exposure and cognitive processing therapy in a VA outpatient clinic. *Psychological Trauma: Theory, Research, Practice, and Policy, 8,* 107–114. http://dx.doi.org/10.1037/tra0000065

Kessler, R. C., Berglund, P., Demler, O., Jin, R., Merikangas, K. R., & Walters, E. E. (2005). Lifetime prevalence and age-of-onset distributions of *DSM–IV* disorders in the National Comorbidity Survey Replication. *Archives of General Psychiatry, 62,* 593–602. http://dx.doi.org/10.1001/archpsyc.62.6.593

Kroenke, K., & Spitzer, R. L. (2002). The PHQ–9: A new depression and diagnostic severity measure. *Psychiatric Annals, 32,* 509–515. http://dx.doi.org/10.3928/0048-5713-20020901-06

Kross, E., & Ayduk, O. (2011). Making meaning out of negative experiences by self-distancing. *Current Directions in Psychological Science, 20,* 187–191. http://dx.doi.org/10.1177/0963721411408883

Kross, E., & Ayduk, O. (2017). Self-distancing: Theory, research and current directions. In J. Olson (Ed.), *Advances in experimental social psychology* (Vol. 55, pp. 81–136). San Diego, CA: Elsevier Academic Press.

Kubany, E. S., Hill, E. E., Owens, J. A., Iannce-Spencer, C., McCaig, M. A., Tremayne, K. J., & Williams, P. L. (2004). Cognitive trauma therapy for battered women with PTSD (CTT-BW). *Journal of Consulting and Clinical Psychology, 72*, 3–18. http://dx.doi.org/10.1037/0022-006X.72.1.3

Lange, A., Rietdijk, D., Hudcovicova, M., van de Ven, J. P., Schrieken, B., & Emmelkamp, P. M. G. (2003). Interapy: A controlled randomized trial of the standardized treatment of posttraumatic stress through the internet. *Journal of Consulting and Clinical Psychology, 71*, 901–909. http://dx.doi.org/10.1037/0022-006X.71.5.901

Lee, C. W., Taylor, G., & Drummond, P. D. (2006). The active ingredient in EMDR: Is it traditional exposure or dual focus of attention? *Clinical Psychology & Psychotherapy, 13*, 97–107. http://dx.doi.org/10.1002/cpp.479

Lindauer, R. J., Gersons, B. P., van Meijel, E. P., Blom, K., Carlier, I. V., Vrijlandt, I., & Olff, M. (2005). Effects of brief eclectic psychotherapy in patients with posttraumatic stress disorder: Randomized clinical trial. *Journal of Traumatic Stress, 18*, 205–212. http://dx.doi.org/10.1002/jts.20029

Management of Posttraumatic Stress Disorder Work Group. (2017). *VA/DoD clinical practice guideline for the management of post-traumatic stress and acute stress reactions.* Washington, DC: Department of Veterans Affairs and Department of Defense. Retrieved from https://www.healthquality.va.gov/guidelines/MH/ptsd/

Marques, L., Robinaugh, D. J., LeBlanc, N. J., & Hinton, D. (2011). Cross-cultural variations in the prevalence and presentation of anxiety disorders. *Expert Review of Neurotherapeutics, 11*, 313–322. http://dx.doi.org/10.1586/ern.10.122

Marx, B. P., Sloan, D. M., Lee, D. J., & Resick, P. A. (2017, November). Moderators of PTSD treatment outcome: Findings from a noninferiority trial. In D. M. Sloan (Chair), *A randomized controlled trial of written exposure therapy for PTSD: Outcomes, moderators, and mediators.* Symposium presented at the 51st annual convention of the Association for Behavioral and Cognitive Therapies, San Diego, CA.

McLean, C. P., Su, Y. J., & Foa, E. B. (2015). Mechanisms of symptom reduction in a combined treatment for comorbid posttraumatic stress disorder and alcohol dependence. *Journal of Consulting and Clinical Psychology, 83*, 655–661. http://dx.doi.org/10.1037/ccp0000024

McLean, C. P., Yeh, R., Rosenfield, D., & Foa, E. B. (2015). Changes in negative cognitions mediate PTSD symptom reductions during client-centered therapy and prolonged exposure for adolescents. *Behaviour Research and Therapy, 68*, 64–69. http://dx.doi.org/10.1016/j.brat.2015.03.008

Nacasch, N., Huppert, J. D., Su, Y. J., Kivity, Y., Dinshtein, Y., Yeh, R., & Foa, E. B. (2015). Are 60-minute prolonged exposure sessions with 20-minute imaginal exposure to traumatic memories sufficient to successfully treat PTSD? A randomized noninferiority clinical trial. *Behavior Therapy, 46*, 328–341. http://dx.doi.org/10.1016/j.beth.2014.12.002

Pagura, J., Stein, M. B., Bolton, J. M., Cox, B. J., Grant, B., & Sareen, J. (2010). Comorbidity of borderline personality disorder and posttraumatic stress disorder in the U.S. population. *Journal of Psychiatric Research, 44*, 1190–1198. http://dx.doi.org/10.1016/j.jpsychires.2010.04.016

Pennebaker, J. W., & Beall, S. K. (1986). Confronting a traumatic event: Toward an understanding of inhibition and disease. *Journal of Abnormal Psychology, 95*, 274–281. http://dx.doi.org/10.1037/0021-843X.95.3.274

Pietrzak, R. H., Goldstein, R. B., Southwick, S. M., & Grant, B. F. (2011). Prevalence and Axis I comorbidity of full and partial posttraumatic stress disorder in the United States: Results from Wave 2 of the National Epidemiologic Survey on Alcohol and Related Conditions. *Journal of Anxiety Disorders, 25*, 456–465. http://dx.doi.org/10.1016/j.janxdis.2010.11.010

Resick, P. A., Galovski, T. E., Uhlmansiek, M. O., Scher, C. D., Clum, G. A., & Young-Xu, Y. (2008). A randomized clinical trial to dismantle components of cognitive processing therapy for posttraumatic stress disorder in female victims of interpersonal violence. *Journal of Consulting and Clinical Psychology, 76*, 243–258. http://dx.doi.org/10.1037/0022-006X.76.2.243

Resick, P. A., Monson, C. M., & Chard, K. M. (2014). *Cognitive processing therapy: Veteran/military version: Therapist and client materials manual.* Washington, DC: Department of Veterans Affairs.

Resick, P. A., Monson, C. M., & Chard, K. M. (2016). *Cognitive processing therapy for PTSD: A comprehensive manual.* New York, NY: Guilford Press.

Resick, P. A., Nishith, P., Weaver, T. L., Astin, M. C., & Feuer, C. A. (2002). A comparison of cognitive-processing therapy with prolonged exposure and a waiting condition for the treatment of chronic posttraumatic stress disorder in female rape victims. *Journal of Consulting and Clinical Psychology, 70*, 867–879. http://dx.doi.org/10.1037/0022-006X.70.4.867

Roberts, A. L., Gilman, S. E., Breslau, J., Breslau, N., & Koenen, K. C. (2011). Race/ethnic differences in exposure to traumatic events, development of post-traumatic stress disorder, and treatment-seeking for post-traumatic stress disorder in the United States. *Psychological Medicine, 41*, 71–83. http://dx.doi.org/10.1017/S0033291710000401

Schnurr, P. P., & Green, B. L. (Eds.). (2004). *Trauma and health: Physical health consequences of exposure to extreme stress.* Washington, DC: American Psychological Association. http://dx.doi.org/10.1037/10723-000

Seedat, S., Scott, K. M., Angermeyer, M. C., Berglund, P., Bromet, E. J., Brugha, T. S., . . . Kessler, R. C. (2009). Cross-national associations between gender and mental disorders in the World Health Organization World Mental Health Surveys. *Archives of General Psychiatry, 66*, 785–795. http://dx.doi.org/10.1001/archgenpsychiatry.2009.36

Shapiro, F. (1989). Eye movement desensitization: A new treatment for post-traumatic stress disorder. *Journal of Behavior Therapy and Experimental Psychiatry, 20*, 211–217. http://dx.doi.org/10.1016/0005-7916(89)90025-6

Sloan, D. M., & Epstein, E. M. (2005). Respiratory sinus arrhythmia predicts written disclosure outcome. *Psychophysiology, 42,* 611–615. http://dx.doi.org/10.1111/j.1469-8986.2005.347.x

Sloan, D. M., Lee, D., Litwack, S., Sawyer, A. T., & Marx, B. P. (2013). Written exposure therapy for veterans diagnosed with PTSD: A pilot study. *Journal of Traumatic Stress, 26,* 776–779. http://dx.doi.org/10.1002/jts.21858

Sloan, D. M., & Marx, B. P. (2004). A closer examination of the structured written disclosure procedure. *Journal of Consulting and Clinical Psychology, 72,* 165–175. http://dx.doi.org/10.1037/0022-006X.72.2.165

Sloan, D. M., & Marx, B. P. (2017). Commentary on the implementation of Written Exposure Therapy (WET) for veterans diagnosed with PTSD. *Pragmatic Case Studies in Psychotherapy, 13,* 154–164.

Sloan, D. M., Marx, B. P., Bovin, M. J., Feinstein, B. A., & Gallagher, M. W. (2012). Written exposure as an intervention for PTSD: A randomized clinical trial with motor vehicle accident survivors. *Behaviour Research and Therapy, 50,* 627–635. http://dx.doi.org/10.1016/j.brat.2012.07.001

Sloan, D. M., Marx, B. P., & Epstein, E. M. (2005). Further examination of the exposure model underlying the efficacy of written emotional disclosure. *Journal of Consulting and Clinical Psychology, 73,* 549–554. http://dx.doi.org/10.1037/0022-006X.73.3.549

Sloan, D. M., Marx, B. P., Epstein, E. M., & Dobbs, J. L. (2008). Expressive writing buffers against maladaptive rumination. *Emotion, 8,* 302–306. http://dx.doi.org/10.1037/1528-3542.8.2.302

Sloan, D. M., Marx, B. P., Epstein, E. M., & Lexington, J. M. (2007). Does altering the writing instructions influence outcome associated with written disclosure? *Behavior Therapy, 38,* 155–168. http://dx.doi.org/10.1016/j.beth.2006.06.005

Sloan, D. M., Marx, B. P., & Greenberg, E. M. (2011). A test of written emotional disclosure as an intervention for posttraumatic stress disorder. *Behaviour Research and Therapy, 49,* 299–304. http://dx.doi.org/10.1016/j.brat.2011.02.001

Sloan, D. M., Marx, P. B., & Lee, D. J. (2018). Written exposure therapy vs. cognitive processing therapy—Reply. *JAMA Psychiatry, 75,* 758–759. http://dx.doi.org/10.1001/jamapsychiatry.2018.0813

Sloan, D. M., Marx, B. P., Lee, D. J., & Resick, P. A. (2018). A brief exposure-based treatment vs. cognitive processing therapy for posttraumatic stress disorder: A randomized noninferiority clinical trial. *JAMA Psychiatry, 75,* 233–239. http://dx.doi.org/10.1001/jamapsychiatry.2017.4249

Sloan, D. M., Marx, B. P., & Resick, P. A. (2016). Brief treatment for PTSD: A non-inferiority trial. *Contemporary Clinical Trials, 48,* 76–82. http://dx.doi.org/10.1016/j.cct.2016.04.003

Smyth, J. M., & Pennebaker, J. W. (2016). *Opening up by writing it down: How expressive writing improves health and eases emotional pain* (3rd ed.). New York, NY: Guilford Press.

Spitzer, R. L., Williams, J. B., Gibbon, M., & First, M. B. (1994). *Structured clinical interview for* DSM–IV—*Client edition*. New York: New York State Psychiatric Institute, Biometrics Research Department.

Spottswood, M., Davydow, D. S., & Huang, H. (2017). The prevalence of posttraumatic stress disorder in primary care: A systematic review. *Harvard Review of Psychiatry, 25*, 159–169. http://dx.doi.org/10.1097/HRP.0000000000000136

Steenkamp, M. M., Litz, B. T., Hoge, C. W., & Marmar, C. R. (2015). Psychotherapy for military-related PTSD: A review of randomized clinical trials. *JAMA, 314*, 489–500. http://dx.doi.org/10.1001/jama.2015.8370

Stein, D. J., Koenen, K. C., Friedman, M. J., Hill, E., McLaughlin, K. A. Petukhova, M., . . . Kessler, R. C. (2013). Dissociation in posttraumatic stress disorder: Evidence from the world mental health surveys. *Biological Psychiatry, 73*, 302–312. http://dx.doi.org/10.1016/j.biopsych.2012.08.022

Stenmark, H., Catani, C., Neuner, F., Elbert, T., & Holen, A. (2013). Treating PTSD in refugees and asylum seekers within the general health care system. A randomized controlled multicenter study. *Behaviour Research and Therapy, 51*, 641–647. http://dx.doi.org/10.1016/j.brat.2013.07.002

Tanielian, T., & Jaycox, L. H. (2008). *Invisible wounds of war: Psychological and cognitive injuries, their consequences, and services to assist recovery*. Santa Monica, CA: RAND Corporation.

Thompson-Hollands, J., Marx, B. P., Lee, D. J., Resick, P. A., & Sloan, D. M. (2018). Long-term treatment gains of a brief exposure-based treatment for PTSD. *Depression and Anxiety, 35*, 985–991. http://dx.doi.org/10.1002/da.22825

van Minnen, A., & Foa, E. B. (2006). The effect of imaginal exposure length on outcome of treatment for PTSD. *Journal of Traumatic Stress, 19*, 427–438.

van Minnen, A., Harned, M. S., Zoellner, L., & Mills, K. (2012). Examining potential contraindications for prolonged exposure therapy for PTSD. *European Journal of Psychotraumatology, 3*, 18805. http://dx.doi.org/10.3402/ejpt.v3i0.18805

van Minnen, A., Zoellner, L. A., Harned, M. S., & Mills, K. (2015). Changes in comorbid conditions after prolonged exposure for PTSD: A literature review. *Current Psychiatry Reports, 17*, 17. http://dx.doi.org/10.1007/s11920-015-0549-1

Watson, J. P., & Marks, I. M. (1971). Relevant and irrelevant fear in flooding: A crossover study of phobic clients. *Behavior Therapy, 2*, 275–293. http://dx.doi.org/10.1016/S0005-7894(71)80062-X

Watts, B. V., Shiner, B., Zubkoff, L., Carpenter-Song, E., Ronconi, J. M., & Coldwell, C. M. (2014). Implementation of evidence-based psychotherapies for posttraumatic stress disorder in VA specialty clinics. *Psychiatric Services, 65*, 648–653. http://dx.doi.org/10.1176/appi.ps.201300176

Weathers, F. W., Blake, D. D., Schnurr, P. P., Kaloupek, D. G., Marx, B. P., & Keane, T. M. (2013a). *The Clinician Administered PTSD Scale for* DSM–5 *(CAPS-5)*. Instrument available from the National Center for PTSD at http://www.ptsd.va.gov

Weathers, F. W., Blake, D. D., Schnurr, P. P., Kaloupek, D. G., Marx, B. P., & Keane, T. M. (2013b). *The Life Events Checklist for* DSM–5 *(LEC-5)*. Instrument available from the National Center for PTSD at http://www.ptsd.va.gov

Weathers, F. W., Bovin, M. J., Lee, D. J., Sloan, D. M., Schnurr, P. P., Kaloupek, D. G., . . . Marx, B. P. (2018). The Clinician-Administered PTSD Scale for *DSM–5* (CAPS-5): Development and initial psychometric evaluation in military veterans. *Psychological Assessment, 30*, 383–395. http://dx.doi.org/10.1037/pas0000486

Weathers, F. W., Keane, T. M., & Davidson, J. T. (2001). Clinician-administered PTSD Scale: A review of the first ten years. *Depression and Anxiety, 13*, 132–156.

Weathers, F. W., Litz, B. T., Herman, D. S., Huska, J. A., & Keane, T. M. (1993, October). *The PTSD checklist (PCL): Reliability, validity, and diagnostic utility*. Poster presented at the 9th annual meeting of the International Society for Traumatic Stress Studies, San Antonio, TX.

Weathers, F. W., Litz, B. T., Keane, T. M., Palmieri, P. A., Marx, B. P., & Schnurr, P. P. (2013). *The PTSD Checklist for* DSM–5 *(PCL-5)*. Retrieved from the National Center for PTSD at http://www.ptsd.va.gov

Wisco, B. E., Baker, A. S., & Sloan, D. M. (2016). Mechanisms of change in written exposure treatment of posttraumatic stress disorder. *Behavior Therapy, 47*, 66–74. http://dx.doi.org/10.1016/j.beth.2015.09.005

Wisco, B. E., Marx, B. P., Wolf, E. J., Miller, M. W., Southwick, S. M., & Pietrzak, R. H. (2014). Posttraumatic stress disorder in the US veteran population: Results from the National Health and Resilience in Veterans Study. *The Journal of Clinical Psychiatry, 75*, 1338–1346. http://dx.doi.org/10.4088/JCP.14m09328

Wolf, E. J., & Schnurr, P. P. (2016). Posttraumatic stress disorder-related cardio-vascular disease and accelerated cellular aging. *Psychiatric Annals, 46*, 527–532. https://dx.doi.org/10.3928/00485713-20160729-01

Wolpe, J. (1958). *Psychotherapy by reciprocal inhibition*. Stanford, CA: Stanford University Press.

World Health Organization. (2018). *ICD–11 for mortality and morbidity statistics*. Retrieved from https://icd.who.int/browse11/l-m/en

Zalta, A. K., Gillihan, S. J., Fisher, A. J., Mintz, J., McLean, C. P., Yehuda, R., & Foa, E. B. (2014). Change in negative cognitions associated with PTSD predicts symptom reduction in prolonged exposure. *Journal of Consulting and Clinical Psychology, 82*, 171–175. http://dx.doi.org/10.1037/a0034735

Index

About the Authors

Denise M. Sloan, PhD, is the associate director of the Behavioral Science Division, National Center for PTSD at VA Boston Healthcare System and a professor of psychiatry at Boston University School of Medicine. Dr. Sloan is a Fellow of the American Psychological Association and the Association for Cognitive and Behavioral Therapies. She graduated with Honors in Psychology from the State University of New York at Stony Brook and earned her doctorate in clinical psychology from Case Western Reserve University.

Dr. Sloan is an expert on psychosocial interventions for traumatic stress disorders with a specific interest in efficient treatment approaches for traumatic stress disorders. Her work has been funded by several organizations, including the National Institute of Mental Health, the Department of Defense, and the Department of Veteran Affairs. She has published over 100 journal articles and has coedited two books. She serves as editor of *Behavior Therapy* and is a consulting editor for six scientific journals.

Brian P. Marx, PhD, is the deputy director of the Behavioral Science Division, National Center for PTSD at VA Boston Healthcare System, and a professor of psychiatry at Boston University School of Medicine. He is a Fellow of the American Psychological Association. Dr. Marx graduated with Honors in Psychology from Boston University in 1989. He completed his doctorate in clinical psychology from the University of Mississippi.

Dr. Marx is an expert in behavior therapy, PTSD assessment, and the effects of trauma. His research interests include the assessment and treatment of PTSD, the identification of risk factors for posttraumatic difficulties, and suicide risk detection and prevention among veterans. His research has received funding from several federal agencies. Dr. Marx has published over 170 journal articles and serves on the editorial boards of several scientific journals. He coauthored *Making Cognitive-Behavioral Therapy Work*, which is now in its third edition.